The Nature, Estimation, and Management of Political Risk

The Nature, Estimation, and Management of Political Risk

Janice Monti-Belkaoui
AND Ahmed Riahi-Belkaoui

QUORUM BOOKS
Westport, Connecticut • London

658.049
M79n

Library of Congress Cataloging-in-Publication Data

Monti-Belkaoui, Janice.
The nature, estimation, and management of political risk / Janice
Monti-Belkaoui and Ahmed Riahi-Belkaoui.
    p. cm.
Includes bibliographical references and index.
ISBN 1–56720–196–2 (alk. paper)
    1. International business enterprises—Management. 2. Country
risk. I. Riahi-Belkaoui, Ahmed, 1943– II. Title.
HD62.4.M65 1998
658'.049—dc21   98–5287

British Library Cataloguing in Publication Data is available.

Library of Congress Catalog Card Number: 98–5287
ISBN: 1–56720–196–2

First published in 1998

Quorum Books, 88 Post Road West, Westport, CT 06881
An imprint of Greenwood Publishing Group, Inc.

Printed in the United States of America

The paper used in this book complies with the
Permanent Paper Standard issued by the National
Information Standards Organization (Z39.48–1984).

10 9 8 7 6 5 4 3 2 1

To Hedi

Contents

Exhibits

Preface

The most serious risk faced by multinational corporations is political risk, as it can result in various negative host government actions that include among others confiscation, expropriation, nationalization, and domestic and creeping expropriation. Management of multinational corporations need to understand the real nature of political risk, use forecasting models to estimate it, and develop alternative measures to manage it. It is exactly the objective of this book to offer theoretical and empirical lenses for viewing the nature of political risk, explaining and predicting political risk, and finally managing it. The tasks are accomplished in five chapters that include an examination of the overall environment of international business most conducive to the rise of political risk (Chapter 1); an examination of the economic environment and the aspects of it most associated with political risk (Chapter 2); an examination of the nature and forecasting models of political risk offered in the literature and in practice (Chapter 3); a determination of a forecasting model that can be used for an explanation and prediction of political risk (Chapter 4); and a presentation of alternative measures for the management of risk (Chapter 5).

This book should be of interest to executives of multinational corporations, management accountants, and students and researchers in international business, finance, marketing, and accounting.

Many people have helped in the development of this book. We received considerable assistance from the University of Illinois at Chicago research assistants, especially Dimitra Alvertos, Saras Natarajan, Belia Ortega, and Erica Sandstrom. We also thank Eric Valentine and the entire production team at Quorum Books for their continuous and intelligent support. Finally, to our entire family, thanks for making everything possible and enjoyable.

The Nature, Estimation, and Management of Political Risk

1

The Overall Environment for International Business and Political Risk

INTRODUCTION

Political risk is a phenomenon faced by multinational firms operating in foreign countries and is associated with various host government actions that include among others confiscation, expropriation, nationalization, domestication, and creeping expropriation.[1] It can also materialize in the forms of general instability risk, ownership/control risk, operation risk, and transfer risk.[2] Other more common risks include exchange controls, price controls, labor problems, tax controls, labor-content laws, and import restrictions. A good appreciation of the potential for political risk demands a thorough appreciation of the new environment for international business in general and the economic environment in particular. This chapter elaborates on the new environment for international business, while Chapter 2 elaborates on the economic environment. The new environment for international business includes (a) special environmental factors proper to the emerging global economy, (b) specific factors of importance to assessing the political environment, and (c) the special situation of the developing world and of capitalism. They are examined next.

ENVIRONMENTAL FACTORS

Global Economy

The global economy is best characterized by a new economic and corporate world in which national boundaries are losing their importance. Emerging characteristics of this global economy include the following.

1. Partnerships are forming between firms of different nationalities, willing to forget their rivalries in order to share in the profit opportunities of a world market; to share the material and labor costs and risks associated with the development of products; to reduce the impact of fluctuating currencies around the world; and to avoid protectionism and government-imposed obstacles such as tariffs, import limits, and regulations. The most noticeable global strategy emanating from these partnerships is the desire to be present in three major markets—Japan, the United States, and Europe—a strategy labeled "triad power," consisting of allocating manufacturing, marketing, financing, and administrative operations among the three markets.

2. Progress is taking place toward international integration in the form of a global capital market. The obstacles to the global capital market remain the persistent existence of different rules concerning regulation of stocks, voting rights, corporate control, anti-trust policies, and accounting policies, to name only a few. As more harmonization takes place among nations, the globalization of stocks and commodities will flourish. One evidence of increased globalization relates to the increasing number of stock markets—by 1992, there were almost two per time zone. The three most important markets, forming what is known as the "golden triangle," are the New York Stock Exchange (NYSE), the London Stock Exchange (LSE), and the Tokyo Stock Exchange (TSE). These markets open at different times, allowing the great trading houses—Merrill Lynch and Solomon Bros. in the United States; Nomura Securities International, Inc., in Japan; and Barclays Bank, PLC, in the United Kingdom—to trade

stocks, bonds, and currencies around the clock and around the world.

3. The rise of the global economy is also evident in the increase in commodity trades and, especially, the creation of big trading blocs. The world seems to be edging toward the following trading blocs:

a. In North America, a trading bloc was created by the signing of the North American Free Trade Agreement in 1992, by the United States, Canada, and Mexico.

b. In Central and South America, trading blocs have been created by (i) the Andean Pact, signed in 1991 by Colombia, Ecuador, Bolivia, Peru, and Venezuela; and (ii) the Mercosur Pact, signed in 1991 by Argentina, Brazil, Paraguay, and Uruguay.

c. In Europe, blocs were created by (i) the establishment of the European Community (EC) in 1957 and now consisting of Belgium, Britain, Denmark, France, Germany, Greece, the Netherlands, Ireland, Italy, Luxembourg, Portugal and Spain, and (ii) the European Free Trade Association (EFTA) set up in 1960 by Liechtenstein, Switzerland, Sweden, Finland, Norway, Iceland, and Austria.

d. In Southeast Asia, a bloc was created by the Association of Southeast Asian Nations Free Trade Area, signed in 1992 by Thailand, Indonesia, Malaysia, the Philippines, Singapore, and Brunei. Vietnam and Laos have also expressed interest in joining the pact.

e. In Africa, a bloc was created by the *Maghreb* countries, an agreement having been signed by Morocco, Algeria, Tunisia, Mauritania, and Libya.

The North American Free Trade Agreement, between the United States, Mexico, and Canada, was announced in August 1992 as the world's largest trading bloc. The agreement is intended to liberalize trade and investment throughout North America.

All these regional trade agreements are the subject of intense debate. Some subscribe to the idea that these arrangements may lead to (a) an undermining of global free-trade negotiations under the General Agreement on Tariffs and Trade, the 103-nation pact that has set the world's free-trade rules since 1947, and (b) an increase in protectionism as countries use regional agreements to steer business toward their allies, instead of buying from whatever country produces most cheaply.

Some, however, feel that regional free-trade deals are better than no free trade at all, forcing some countries to open their markets to foreign products.

4. In addition to these trading blocs, new economic powers are emerging, especially Japan and the newly unified Germany, to compete head-on with the United States.

The key words arising from this new economic order are *competitiveness* and *survival*. A new paradigm maintains that competitiveness itself motivates the success of nations. Such is the thesis of Porter, who maintains that the ability of a nation to upgrade its existing advantages to the next level of technology and productivity is the key to international success.[3] Four factors, called the ''diamond'' of national competitive advantages, are presented as the key to the success of nations:

1. Factor conditions (a nation's ability to turn factor endowment into a specialized advantage);
2. Demand conditions (the existence of demanding, sophisticated customers);
3. Related and supporting industries that provide supplies clusters to firms; and
4. Company, strategy, structure, and rivalry (conditions governing how firms in a nation are created and nurtured during times of intense competition).

The differences in competitiveness internationally may be attributed to the differences in corporate ownership and corporate objectives in various parts of the world. In the United States, for example, transient owners such as institutional investors, pension funds, mutual funds, and money managers focus on short-term objectives rather than long-term growth. A 1992 examination of statistics from the stock exchanges in the United States, Japan, and Germany revealed the following differences in corporate ownership:

	US	Japan	Germany
Individuals	30-35%	20%	4%
Institutional owners	2%	40%	27%
Institutional agents	55-60%	6%	3%
Corporations	2-7%	30%	41%
Government	Negligible	Negligible	6%
Foreign investors	6%	4%	19%

Similarly, a 1992 survey by Japan's Economic Planning Agency of 1,000 U.S. and 1,000 Japanese companies revealed the following differences in corporate objectives (the ranking of corporate objectives varies from 3 = most important to 0 = least important):

	US	Japan
Return on investment	2.43	1.24
Higher stock prices	1.14	0.02
Market shares	0.73	1.43
Improving products and introducing new products	0.71	1.54
Streamlining production and distributing systems	0.46	0.71
Net worth ratio	0.38	0.59
Improvement of social image	0.05	0.20
Improvement of working conditions	0.04	0.09

It appears that the American system of capital allocation relies heavily on external capital provided by transient owners comprised of institutional investors, pension funds, mutual funds, and other money managers who are mainly interested in short-term gains. These owners/agents are very motivated by the market performance of their stocks, at the expense of direct interest in the company, its goals, or its level of international competitiveness. As a result, American managers place a higher focus on earning high returns on investments and maximizing current stock prices.

The external and internal capital allocation systems are different in Japan and Germany, where rather than agents the dominant owners are principals, who seek long-term growth and have a special relationship with the firm. This special relationship translates into access to inside information, and greater influence on managerial behavior.

The Role of the Multinational Corporation

Mueller gives the following accurate characterization of the multinational corporations:

The international corporation is emerging. This is a corporation that is internationally owned and controlled. It is not a domestic corporation with some foreign business. It is a business organization with a truly international organization for all its business functions, including management, production, marketing and finance.[4]

It is generally a domestic firm that expanded for the development of a strong product for domestic sales to a complex firm with a multinational management organization and a multinational ownership of equity securities.

It can take one of two forms:

1. *A world corporation format* that includes the merger of domestic and foreign operations for the functions of research and development, manufacturing, marketing, and finance; or

2. *An international division format*, where all foreign operations are separated from their domestic counterparts in an international division.[5]

The multinational corporation (MNC) is best viewed as a collection of valuable options.[6] Various benefits can be achieved through the MNC:

1. Significant arbitrage benefits can be obtained through:

a. exploitation of financing bargains;
b. reduction of taxes on financial flows;
c. the mitigation or shifting of risks to agents with a comparative advantage in bearing them;
d. diversification of cash flows received through foreign operations;
e. the exploitation of various institutional perfections; and
f. the capturing and appropriation of information.

2. Foreign operating options allow additional benefits through:

a. *location options*, which are associated with location alternatives that enhance profits;
b. *timing options*, which are connected with the exploitation of transient costs and exchange rate disparities;
c. *technology options*, linking international cost disparities and flexible technologies for the exploitation of the short-term price changes; and
d. *staging options*, which are associated with establishing a discernible presence in foreign markets.[7]

3. Other benefits include capital availability and a desirable cost of capital for a considerable range of its capital budget.[8]

The multinational corporation's objective is to maximize shareholder wealth, subject to environmental, regulatory, and ethical constraints. The objective is sometimes difficult to achieve if managers decide to maximize their own utility functions. This is the *agency problem*, where the goals of shareholders conflict with those of the managers. The problem may be more frequent in the case of multinational corporations, where managers of different subsidiaries are more inclined to maximize the value of their respective subsidiaries. The multinational corporation calls for specific performance evaluation and control techniques to alleviate the potential agency problems that arise from the divergent interests of subsidiaries and the multinational corporation. It also calls for specific accounting standards to deal with unique pressures of accountability from domestic and foreign interest groups. Accordingly, Gray et al. argued that there is a case for standards applicable to multinational corporations as follows:

The present lack of consistency in MNC accountability and the proliferation of national standards may lead to the conclusion that worldwide harmonization of MNC reporting—disclosure and measurement—is needed. Equally, there may be a major priority for international (domestic) enterprises with no foreign operations, because the needs of the international investment community, the main agency involved and relatively expert, could be met to a large extent by accounting policy disclosures. It is only then international companies become units of a supernatural economic ability, the MNC, that arguments of consistency and comparability in the interests of international constituencies of users become persuasive.[9]

Foreign Direct Investment

Foreign direct investment involves the transfer of capital, managerial, and technical assets of a firm from one country (the home country) to another (the host country) by (within) the same firm. Firms engage in foreign direct investment and expand their markets by producing and selling abroad. Some reasons include the following:

- To reduce transportation costs;
- Because of a lack of domestic policy;
- To achieve economies of scale in small-scale process technology;
- To avoid trade or customer-imposed restrictions;
- To follow customers and competitors;
- To benefit from a different cost structure;
- To achieve some vertical integration;
- To rationalize production by taking advantage of varying costs of labor, capital, and raw materials;

- To have access to production factors;
- To take advantage of government investment incentives;
- Because of political motives;
- To use a monopoly advantage over similar companies in the foreign countries; and
- To have better profitability and stable sales and earnings.[10,11]

Various models and theories can be used to explain foreign direct investment (FDI). They include international trade theory, the location theory, the investment theory, the theory of the firm, and the industrial organization theory.

The International Monetary System

The international monetary system (IMS) constitutes the structure within which exchange rates are determined, international trade and capital flows are accumulated, and balance-of-payments adjustments are made. To better appreciate the exchange rate problem and how it affects international accounting practices, a good grasp of the IMS is essential.

The United Nations Monetary and Financial Conference held in Bretton Woods, New Hampshire, in 1944, with the objective of developing an IMS, created both the International Monetary Fund (IMF), and the International Bank for Reconstruction and Development, known as the World Bank. The IMF's objectives set by the charter are:

1. To promote international monetary cooperation . . . through consultation and collaboration;
2. To facilitate the expansion and balanced growth of international trade;
3. To promote exchange stability . . . and to avoid competitive exchange depreciation;
4. To assist in the establishment of a multilateral system of payments . . . and in the elimination of foreign exchange restrictions; and

5. To give confidence to members by making the Fund's resources available to them . . . thus providing them with opportunity to correct (temporary) maladjustments in their balances of payments.

Soon, the fixed exchange rate system or par value based on gold and the U.S. dollar proved inadequate, and called for improvements. This was accomplished by two actions:

1. Swap agreements, whereby instant reserves were created by a swap of credit lines between central banks, were facilitated; and
2. A more lasting solution to the need for growth in the world monetary reserves was provided, by the creation of a new unit of reserve called the Special Drawing Right (SDR). This system allowed countries to borrow or withdraw SDRs from the IMF to buy other countries' currencies.

However, a crisis in the IMS caused by an overvalued dollar and growing U.S. balance of trade deficits in December 1971 caused the convening of another conference that resulted in the Smithsonian Agreement and the devaluation of the U.S. dollar. A further devaluation of the dollar in 1973 showed the limits of the fixed rate system. From these crises there emerged the following exchange rate systems:

1. *A fixed rate system*, where the value of the currency is "pegged" (fixed) to another currency, or allowed to fluctuate only within very narrow boundaries.

2. *A freely floating exchange rate system*, where the value of the currency is determined by market forces and not through intervention by government.

3. *A managed-float exchange rate system*, where the value of the currency is allowed to fluctuate and governments intervene to ensure the value does not move too much in a given direction. It is also known as a "managed float" or "dirty float."

4. *A pegged exchange rate system*, used by members of the European Community to peg the value of their currencies to a basket of currencies, expressed in ECUs (European Currency

Units), and to limit fluctuations within established limits. The system is also known as the "snake." The 1991 Maastricht Agreement between the members of the European Community is stated to give birth by 1999 to a European Central Bank, a single currency (or national currencies) "irrevocably" fixed with one another, with the provision that the central bank will conduct a single monetary policy.

The World Bank is an international profit-oriented bank whose objective is to make loans to countries for economic development projects, and to secure funds through the sale of bonds and other debt instruments to private investors and governments.

Other institutions include:

1. The International Financial Corporation (IFC), devoted to the promotion of private enterprise within countries;

2. The International Development Association (IDA), devoted to promotion of economic development for very needy nations;

3. The Bank of International Settlements, "a central bank's central bank," devoted to facilitating international transactions among countries; and

4. Regional Development Agencies, devoted to regional economic development, such as
   a. the Inter-American Development Bank,
   b. the Asian Development Bank,
   c. the African Development Fund, and
   d. the European Bank for Reconstruction and Development, to name only a few.

ASSESSING THE POLITICAL ENVIRONMENT

The political dimension of political risk consists of examining the political environment toward an accurate assessment of domestic politics. One approach that can be easily developed with a checklist strategy is to identify the main political variables of risk. For example, Raddock[12] identified the following variables of risk:

1. Leadership succession;
2. Crisis of a legitimacy of a regime;
3. Rising expectations or hopes for social mobility and the frustration thereof;
4. Disaffection of the middle class;
5. Professional support from the regime;
6. Historical propensity to default, nationalize, or expropriate gradually through increased regulations;
7. Corruption;
8. Secular and sacred ideologies;
9. Demographic patterns;
10. Labor agitation and worker participation in management;
11. Cultural, regional, and traditional/modern cleavages in society;
12. Civil disorder, violence, and terrorism;
13. Military unrest;
14. External territorial disputes;
15. Elites and their relative influence;
16. Nationalism and national goals;
17. The reform versus a retrenchment pattern; and
18. Social revolution and living with the winner.

Similarly, Onkivist and Shaw identified the following indicators of political instability: (a) social unrest, (b) attitudes of naturals, and (c) policies of the host government.[13] Alderson[14] and Onkivist and Shaw[15] trace the social unrest nearest to the conflict between monostasy (the urge to stand alone) with its focus on competition, and systasy (the urge to stand together) with its focus on cooperation. The modernization and competition effort since the breakup of the Soviet Union led to a shift toward monostasy with the resulting urge of ethnic groups to seek autonomy and freedom. Social unrest is also the result of economic, religious, racial, and cultural factors.

The best way of assessing the political environment may be

(a) a good comprehension of the ideological forces at work, (b) an analysis of foreign policy, and (c) an understanding of the approaches to politics.

Ideological Forces

A way of assessing the stability of the political environment in general and political risk in particular is to have a good appreciation of the ideological forces that are shaping governmental policies and that are used to define the national interest. An excellent definition of ideology follows:

> An ideology is a value system or belief system accepted as fact or truth by some group. It is composed of a set of attitudes toward the various institutions and processes of society. An ideology provides the believer with a picture of the world both as it is and as it should be, and, in doing so, organizes the tremendous complexity of the world into something simple and understandable.[16]

There are, however, hundreds of ideologies and versions of ideologies. Those that are most likely to influence political risk are explicated next.

1. *Liberalism* in the twentieth-century United States is an ideology that favors greater government participation in the economy and regulation or ownership of business. Liberals hold the belief that government should:

- Actively undertake to reduce poverty;
- Ensure at least adequate levels of health, safety, and economic security;
- *Not* interfere with a woman's reproductive freedom;
- Protect the environment; and
- Reduce defense spending in comparison to domestic spending.[17]

2. *Conservatism* in the twentieth-century United States is an ideology that favors minimizing governmental activities in favor

of more activities by private businesses and individuals. In the United States, it is differentiated into three types: (a) classical conservatism, where the best of society is assured be to founded on experience, custom, position, and privilege in a society that maintains order and produces legal, economic, and social systems conducive to harmony and peace;[18] (b) contemporary conservatism, where economically it favors less public spending on social programs in favor of spending on defense, or reducing taxes, and morally, it favors traditional family values;[19] and (c) neoconservatism with its focus on traditional family and religious values, respect for authority, and free market forces.[20]

3. *Communism* is an ideology and a theory of social change, conceived by Karl Marx and arrived at by attaining the objective of a classless society. It is characterized by a public ownership of all economic and social entities.

4. *Totalitarianism* is a political ideology characterized by a monopolization of political power by the state in the case of *communist totalitarianism*, by a party, group, or individual that governs according to religious principles in the case of *theocratic totalitarianism*; by a tribal or ethnic group in the case of *tribal totalitarianism*, and by right-wing dictatorships in the case of *right-wing totalitarianism*.

5. *Fundamentalism* is a religious ideology calling for a return to the ''fundamentals'' of faith, whether it is Islam, Christianity, or Judaism. Fundamentalists share at least three common beliefs:

- Contemporary society is morally corrupt and the source of corruption is identifiable.
- A return to God is necessary.
- The will of God is known through ''the Book,'' which explains God's plan for individuals and society.[21]

6. *Capitalism* is an economic and political ideology that calls for a laissez-faire, free economy dominated by market forces, and restricts government to those functions that the private sector

cannot perform, such as national defense, police, fire, and other public services and foreign policy.

7. *Socialism* is an economic and political ideology that calls for more government ownership or control of the basic means of production, distribution, and exchange. It is generally differentiated with *European socialism* based on social democracy and *less developed countries socialism* based on government's ownership and control of most of the factors of production.

Foreign Policy Analysis

Understanding political analysis and using political models can facilitate the analysis of political sources of risk. These models present different lenses through which the analyst can better view and analyze the nature and determination of various political processes and use a distinctive conceptual approach to political analysis. Different models of politics have been suggested in the literature. They are explicated next.

Brewer's Analytic Models

Brewer suggested 10 models of politics.[22] Four can be used in the analysis of political sources of risk.[23] They are reviewed next.

1. *The state-centric model of international politics* assumes that each country uses its resources and national power capabilities to further its own national interest and agenda in response to the actions and problems posed by other states in the context of a competitive, decentralized international political system. The national governments seek security and status in reaction to political pressures that may be exerted by international crises.

This approach has been criticized as being parochially conservative and advocating unjust status quo. As stated by Brewer:

The international politics model has been criticized for being too narrow empirically. It ignores many significant aspects of contemporary world politics. Indeed, it almost entirely neglects a variety of important

developments in world politics in the past several decades. It exagger-
ates the independence, autonomy, and sovereignty of nation-states. It
underestimates the significance of international organizations and nongovernmental organizations in world politics. It underestimates the importance of economic goals independent of their relationship to national
security and status. It ignores the cooperative aspects of world politics
(except for alliances). Finally, it relies on a narrow notion of power,
with undue emphasis on military focus as a power capability.[24]

2. *The transnational politics model* views the arena of world
politics as the domain not only of national governments but also
of multinational corporations, international organizations, and
nongovernmental associations. The interactions of these actors
across national boundaries is dominated by the search for interest
and power, defining in the process a new transnational interest
groups. A confusing and more complex political environment of
foreign policy making is created limiting the power of national
governments, and shifting the focus from national interests to
various transnational economic activities.

3. *The pluralistic model of national politics* views the politics
adopted by national governments as a response to the diverse
and conflicting interests and pressures of organized interest
groups, pressure groups, or lobbies. One condition for remaining
in power is to be protective of these interests; which given the
diversity of interests leads to policy conflict and to policy making
as a highly politicized resolution process.[25] Official position,
wealth, expertise, political skills, information, and operational
capabilities determine the sources of influence of policy making.

4. *The bureaucratic politics model* views politics adopted by
national governments as a response to organizational processes,
repertoires, and political tactics within governmental bureaucra-
cies. As stated by Brewer:

Intra-governmental conflicts are generated, for instance, by the differing
policy preferences of individual officials and agencies which arise from

their conflicting organizational interests, differences in their career experiences, differences in their ties to domestic clientele groups, and other factors. This model also suggests that government policies are slow to change because of bureaucratic inertia.[26]

Allison's Essence of a Decision

Another framework of analysis is the series of conceptual models developed by Allison in his *Essence of a Decision*, namely Model I, Model II, and Model III.[27] In what follows, each of the models is explained. A critical evaluation of the Allison approach is then presented.

The Rational Actor Approach. Allison's Model I is the *rational actor* model. It takes as its basic unit of analysis the organization's action as rational choice. The action or choice it makes amounts to a maximization of the goals, values, and objectives. It is a rational choice in the sense that it "consists of value-maximizing adaptation within the context of a *given* payoff function, *fixed* alternatives, and consequences that are *known*."[28]

The rational choice can be an optimal choice given an assumption of comprehensive rationality when the decision maker knows totally the payoff function by an accurate mapping of all the consequences in terms of the agent's value, all the alternatives, and all the consequences.[29] A sure acceptable assumption would be, of course, the one of limited rationality restricting clauses of optimal choice. To use the "rational actor" model to explain an organization's action, the analyst identifies the correct goals, alternatives, and consequences by putting himself or herself in the place of the organization.

The Organizational Process Approach. Allison's Model II is the *organizational process* model. What Model I views as "acts" or "choices" are viewed by Model II as "output" of organizations regulated by standard patterns of behavior. The emphasis is the organization's action as organizational output. The action or choice it makes results from some established standard rules, procedures, and repertoires of the organization. As explained by J. D. Cheshire and E. H. Feroz:

The core of this model is the output based on standard operating procedures (SOP). Behavior is predetermined by SOP. Goals are not achieved by maximizing values but by operating within a pre-established set of performance criteria. The process of coordinating past, present and future events to a consistent decision base is an important factor in the model. Another element of the model is that uncertainty is dealt with by conformity. If one is uncertain as to the reliability and consequences of a decision then he/she will conform to the confines of a predetermined organizational standard. The emphasis on conformity in this model does not mean that the decision will not have a sound base. It means that the perspective from which the rationale is drawn is derived from preestablished guidelines as opposed to considering decisions independently and in their own right as in the rational actor model.[30]

The Political Approach. In a Model III analysis, the identification of the perceptions, power, positions, and maneuvers of each of the major players is used to explain the chosen alternatives with each player acting on their own perception of the issue through a psychopolitical bargaining power.

Critical Evaluations. The above analysis has revealed the usefulness and some weaknesses of the use of the Allison approach to an understanding of foreign policy decisions. The decision may be viewed as rational, organizational, or political. The resulting three interpretations could be, however, contradictory or complementary. The analyst may be tempted to choose the political stand that corresponds to either the rational or organizational interpretations.

The above discussion points to major weaknesses of the Allison approach:

1. The first weakness may arise from the possible case where three different interpretations resulted from the three models. In fact, the three different interpretations may be the rule rather than the exception when a multitude of conflicting events preceded the decision, and the analyst has to choose some of those events to use in each model. The choice of what is a relevant event by the analyst may influence the interpretation resulting from each

model. The three interpretations could also be different due to the *units of analysis* but also to differences in the *level of analysis*.

The basic unit of analysis is the foreign policy action as a rational choice for Model I, as organizational output for Model II, and as political resultant for Model III. As admitted by Allison, Models II and III deal with aggregates, while Model I focuses on only a single actor. Consequently, the explanations of the organizational processes and political models will be by definition more elaborate and complex, with less vigor and consistency than the deductive explanation of the rational model. Moreover, the explanation of Models II and III are at a comparatively lower level. Model II, based on the previous repertoires, explains the result only in terms of similarity to previous treatments. Model III explains the result by recounting the parameters of the bargaining game without explaining what causes one player to have more power than another.

2. The second weakness exists principally in the political model. If there is no possible alternative capable of creating a consensus of acceptance between the various players, any choice is a political choice.

3. The third weakness exists in the data collection methodology used in the three models. It is a documentary method based on examination and analysis of the testimony, transcripts, and prepared statements of the participants. For more reliability, it may be possible, and more desirable, to augment this sort of documentary analysis with observational and interview models. In fact, Models II and III may attain a higher level of precision in their explanation if the positions and tactics of the players and the standard operating procedures were uncovered by a field study. Another approach is the idea of a cognitive map of a person's stated values and casual beliefs.[31] There are, however, serious limitations to the cognitive mapping approach, such as the potential for insincerity in policy decisions, the slowness of the documentary coding methods, the absence of any types of relationships in cognitive maps other than casual or value rela-

tionships, and the lack of quantification in the relationships that are represented.[32]

4. Other weaknesses were also reported by Allison when applying the three models to explain the U.S. decision to impose a blockade in Cuba during the Cuban Missile Crisis. For example, Allison had problems in differentiating the Model II from the Model III explanation. Similarly, Chong-Do Hah and Robert M. Lindquist formed the same weakness in applying the Allison's approach to the 1952 steel seizure decision by President Harry Truman.[32] They also attributed the differences in the resulting explanations not only to unit of analysis but also to differences in the level of analysis.[34]

5. Another weakness results from different analysts relying on different dimensions of reality, resulting in different interpretations.

The usefulness of the Allison approach rests on the ability of the analyst to determine the relevant and important dimensions of reality that influenced the final decision and the use of both documentary and observational and interview methods for the data collection. The ability to determine the most relevant events is necessary to ensure the right interpretation by each of the three conceptual models and to comprehend the relations between the various interpretations, whether they are interrelated; whether they shed light on each other; whether they are contradictory, complementary, or part of a larger synthesis; and whether one dominates the other. The additional use of observational and interview methods may help uncover the repertoires used in the organizational model and the parameters of the bargaining game used in the political model. The Allison approach is easily applicable to foreign policy decisions. The final interpretation may rest on the additional use of observational and interview methods.

Approaches to Politics

In assessing the political environment for a determination of political risk the analyst may find himself or herself examining

Exhibit 1.1
Ideological-Methodological Groups

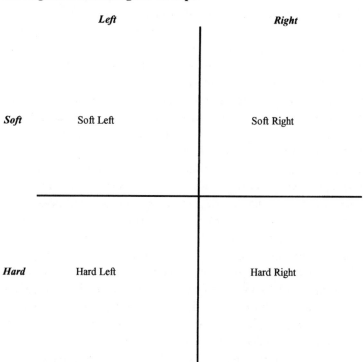

and/or studying political writings. In doing so, he or she may notice the existence of separate schools and the rest in political science, providing different views and interpretations of the same political phenomenon. A typology provided by Almond[35] can facilitate an understanding of the different conceptions of proper political science. His typology divides the discipline in four categories, two ideological (left and right) and two methodological (hard and soft). The resulting ideological-methodological groups, shown in Exhibit 1.1, are (a) the soft left, (b) the soft right, (c) the hard left, and (d) the hard right. The soft-hard methodological dimension differentiates between the soft or descriptive and philosophical methodologies and the hard or quantitative methodologies. The left-right ideological dimension differentiates

between the right with its focus on power and rational thinking
and the left with its focus on social, economic, or political equality. The four groups are explicated next.

1. *The soft left group* with its descriptive and philosophical
methodology and its concern for social, economic, and political
equality, includes feminism, political psychology, and critical
theory. Feminism, as an intellectual perspective and a social
movement, takes either the moderate position of seeking to
broaden the range of opportunities for women or the radical perspective of viewing patriarchy as the most pervasive feature of
social life.[36] Political psychology attempts to use psychological
concepts to gain an understanding of political phenomena.

An example by Barber[37] is the classification of presidents into
personality types whether they are active or passive or possessive
or negative in pursuit of their goals. Critical theory approaches
societal problems with the objective of finding solutions to situations of alienation, inequality, and lack of commitment.

2. *The hard right group*, with its reliance on scientific methodologies and a focus on power and rational thinking, includes
the rational actor theory and decision making analysis,[38] public
choice theory,[39] game theory,[40] systems analysis,[41] structural-
functionalism,[42] and communications theory.[43]

3. *The soft right group*, with its descriptive and philosophical
methodology and its concern for power and natural thinking,
includes traditional political analysis,[44] and studies of the state
of both Strauss[45] and Voegelin.[46]

4. *The hard left group*, with its reliance on scientific methodologies and a focus on social, economic, and political equality,
includes mostly socialist and dependency theories.[47] Their classification of world capitalism as consisting of four interrelated
classes is summarized as follows:

1. The capitalist center (capitalists in the United States, Japan, and
   Western Europe);
2. The periphery of the center (exploited underclasses of the capitalist
   world);

3. The center of the periphery (dependent bourgeoisie in Latin America, Africa, and Third-World countries); and

4. The periphery of the periphery (rural Far Eastern and other peasant populations).[48]

THE SPECIAL SITUATION OF THE DEVELOPING WORLD

Modernized and Modernizing Nations

One classification of forms of government that can be used as a predictor of radical political change is in terms of the level of modernization. Accordingly, Green distinguishes between modernized nations and modernizing nations.[49] Modernizing nations, which include the most economically developed nations, are divided into either (a) the countries possessing governments that behave according to instrumental-adaptive procedures or (b) the countries possessing governments that are governed by instrumental, but nonadaptive regimes, where "instrumental" refers to a democratic system, and "adaptive" refers to responsiveness to the dictates of the policy.[50] Modernizing nations are classified in the following five categories.

a. Instrumental and quasi-instrumental systems attempting adaptive politics. As Green stated: "These nations possess a solid political infrastructure and political institutions which have withstood several crises and have subsequently become involved into the populace. In general, the nations included in this category have had an opportunity to develop their political systems over a long period of time, building upon the structure of their predecessors."[51] Needless to say, these countries present to the businessman the least risk of radical political change.

b. Military dictatorship, reflecting special and difficult social and political conditions. These countries offer to the businessman a huge risk for long-term investment.

c. Modernizing autocracies, ruled by highly centralized civilian regimes such as dictatorial systems, monarchies, and oligarchies.

While they offer the businessman a relatively stable environment, a certain degree of risk exists during periods of succession from one ruler to another.

d. Mobilizing systems, which "are characteristically those which exhibit extreme militarism, devotion to a cause, and usually possess a leader endowed with charisma and super-human qualities."[52] They offer the businessman volatile conditions but also the prospects of promising markets and stable political systems as they evolve toward economic "take-off."[53]

e. Recently-independent nations, which are characterized by a high degree of uncertainty and a certain propensity for radical political change through revolutions. They offer the businessman a relatively high degree of risk and instability.

The Meaning of Development

Developing countries face insurmountable problems in their attempts to achieve progress in their economic development programs. Their efforts have led to the rise of a new economic subdiscipline—namely, development economics—to address the various problems and policies affecting economic development. The problems and policies are either domestic—such as growth, poverty, income distribution, unemployment, population growth, education, agricultural transformation, and rural development— or international—foreign investment and aid, and new international economic order. These problems and policies are examined in this chapter, in addition to an explication of economic development and its contemporary problems.

Two thirds of the world's population subsists on only 20 percent of the world's income. These people live in a state of underdevelopment, forcefully portrayed as follows:

Underdevelopment is shocking: The squalor, disease, unnecessary deaths, and hopelessness of it all! No man understands if underdevelopment remains for him a mere statistic reflecting low income, poor housing, premature mortality and underemployment. The most empathetic observer can speak objectively about underdevelopment only after undergoing, personally or vicariously, the ''shock of underdevelopment.'' This unique culture shock comes to one as he is initiated to the emotions which prevail in the ''culture of poverty.'' The reverse shock is felt by those living in destitution when a new self-understanding reveals to them that their life is neither human nor inevitable . . . the prevalent emotion of underdevelopment is a sense of personal and societal impotence in the face of disease and death, of confusion and ignorance as one probes to understand change, of servility toward men whose decisions govern the course of events, of hopelessness before hunger and natural catastrophe. Chronic poverty is a cruel kind of hell; and one cannot understand how cruel that hell is merely by gazing upon poverty as an object.[54]

These much less fortunate people live in what are generally characterized as developing countries. Various classifications of these countries exist:

1. The UN classifies these countries in three major groups designed as (a) the ''least developed'' for the 42 poorest countries, sometimes referred to as the ''Fourth World''; (b) the ''developing nations'' for the 88 non-oil-exporting countries; and (c) the oil-exporting nations for the 13 members of the Organization of Petroleum Exporting Countries (OPEC).

2. The Organization for Economic Cooperation and Development (OECD) classifies these countries into 62 low-income countries (LICs), 73 middle-income countries (MICs), 11 newly industrialized nations (NICs), and 13 members of OPEC.

3. The World Bank, also known as the International Bank for Reconstruction and Development (IBRD), classifies these developed and developing countries into six categories: low income, middle income, upper middle income, high-income oil exporters, industrial market economies, and East European nonmarket economies.

Whatever the definition adopted, the developing countries share some common characteristics of underdevelopment generally grouped into the following six broad categories:

1. Low levels of living;
2. Low levels of productivity;
3. High rates of population growth and dependency burdens;
4. High and rising levels of unemployment and underemployment;
5. Significant dependence on agricultural production and primary product exports; and
6. Dominance, dependence, and vulnerability in international relations.[55]

The combination of any number of these categories in a given country creates a state of underdevelopment. It is the result of not only economic but also social forces, not only internal but also external factors, and not only national but also international origins. It calls for each of these nations to formulate appropriate strategies of growth and development at the national level and, as seen later, modification of the international economic order at the international level. The basic objective of these strategies would be to break what Gunnar Myrdal refers to as the phenomenon of "circular and cumulative causation generated by the interactions between low levels of living and low productivity."[56]

These strategies have to take into account the structural diversity of the developing nations as exemplified by the following seven major components:

1. The size of the country (geographic, population, and income),
2. Historical evolution,
3. Physical and human resource endowments,
4. The relative importance of public and private sectors,
5. The nature of the industrial structure,
6. The degree of dependence on external economic and political forces, and
7. The distribution of power and the institutional and political structure within the nation.[57]

The study of development economics is a relatively new and separate area in the disciplines of economics and political economy. It deals with the economic, social, and institutional tools necessary to bring changes in the levels of living of developing countries.[58]

Basically, development economics addresses the critical questions about the economies of the developing countries, questions that center on finding the best way—economically, socially, and institutionally—of bringing these countries to an acceptable and decent level of living and productivity. It obviously goes beyond simple economics. In fact, there is an implicit assumption in development economics about the limited relevance of traditional theory. Myrdal states the case as follows:

Economic theorists, more than any other social scientists, have long been disposed to arrive at general propositions and then postulate them as valid for every time, place and culture. There is a tendency in contemporary economic theory to follow this path to the extreme. When theories and concepts designed to fit the special conditions of the Western World—and thus containing the implicit assumptions about social reality by which this fitting was accomplished—are used in the study of underdeveloped countries, where they do *not* fit, the consequences are serious.[59]

The developing countries need to go beyond simple economics and adopt strategies that attack not only economic problems but all other problems of the social systems of their nations. That is the objective of development economics. It goes beyond the formal modeling of conventional economics to cover a more exhaustive approach to development. In effect, formal modeling, by itself, is insufficient to provide a clear picture of poverty. Such a model would not be able to describe adequately the complexity of poverty and its application would not be easy, given the more difficult task of measuring all the required parameters.[60] This model needs to differ from those adopted in developed countries. A new paradigm of economic development, which differs from those adopted for the economic development of the Western countries, is needed as shown by the following arguments:

1. The capital and cultivable land resources available to the underdeveloped countries are much more limited than was the case during Western economic development.

2. Without comparable resources, labor productivity cannot be improved by means similar to those that have been successful in the West.

3. International and domestic demand conditions are such that urban industrialization cannot be expected to grow at a rate that permits the transfer of labor from agriculture into higher productivity urban industrial occupation; at the same time the limited demand conditions also slow down or prevent the adoption of modern agrarian technologies and, hence, prevent the growth of rural income.

4. Urban migration is already in excess of what is economically justified, as shown by the widespread urban unemployment in almost all underdeveloped countries.

5. Social justice and structural conditions in the economy require an improvement in the distribution of income and a growth in the incomes of the lower income groups. But these can be brought about only by increasing employment and work opportunities at higher returns than the market can yield. Since the primary opportunities for the productive use of unskilled labor can be found in rural and agricultural-related activities rather than urban industrial or service employment, the focus of the development effort must be shifted from urban industrialization toward rural transformation. But there are no competitive market processes that can bring about the required change; hence the market must be, in some of its basic functions, replaced by government or community action. Hence the need for a new paradigm for development.[61]

As stated earlier, development is more than an economic process. It involves the economic, social, and institutional processes necessary to efficiently eliminate the major evils of underde-

velopment: malnutrition, disease, illiteracy, slums, unemployment, and inequality. Besides the creation of self-sustained
growth in per capita gross national product (GNP), it involves
the requisite modernization of economic, social, and political
structures implicit in the achievement of GNP growth. The basic
purpose and meaning of development is *depauperization*, which
has been defined as follows:

Depauperization has both economic and noneconomic dimensions and
stresses the removal not only of material but equally importantly of
social, political and spiritual forms of deprivation. It involves not only
equity but more significantly the creation of conditions conducive to
continuing improvements in equity. It may require temporary sacrifices
in national economic growth and involves major social and institutional
changes.[62]

Development calls then for both the elimination of deprivation
and the restoration of equity in addition to the achievement of
GNP growth. Achieving good growth and effectively distributing
the growth is the essence of good development. Development
goals focus on the improvement in human life and human happiness. While human life and/or human happiness are universal
goals and values sought by every developing country, these universal values that all societies desire and that development claims
to foster are life sustenance, self-esteem, and freedom.[63]

Life sustenance includes people's requirement for food, shelter, healing, or survival. Development's main goal is to provide
such life-sustaining goods as food, medicine, adequate shelter,
and protection. As Dennis Goulet states, ''Quite clearly, one of
development's most important goals is to prolong man's lives
and render those men less 'stunted' by disease, extreme exposure
to nature's elements, and defenseless against enemies.''[64]

Self-esteem is every person's sense that he or she has worth,
that he or she is respected and is not used as a tool by others
for their own purposes. In some societies, this self-esteem is
expressed by the need for identity, dignity, respect, honor, or

recognition. The need for self-esteem is a major drive for achieving development. As Goulet states, "Therefore, the conviction is gaining strength throughout the world that mass poverty cuts societies off from due recognition or esteem. Once deprivation of esteem reaches an intolerable point, people are quite ready to begin desiring material 'development.' "[65]

Freedom from any form of servitude to nature, ignorance, other people, institutions, and beliefs is a fundamental goal of and drive for development. With freedom comes development and a great choice for people in dealing with their environment.

Three basic schools of thought dominate the economic development literature: an early literature on the stages of economic growth and more recent literature on the structural change models and the international dependency paradigms.

1. The linear stage of economic growth focuses on the importance to development of both the acquisition and use of capital and the historical development of the developed countries. One example is *Rostow's argument* that the advanced countries have passed the stage of "takeoff into self-sustaining growth," while the underdeveloped countries are in a "precondition" stage, and in need of massive infusion of domestic and foreign savings before growth takes place.[66] A second example is the *Harrod-Domar growth model*, which simply states that the growth of national income will be directly, or positively, related to the savings ratio, and inversely or negatively related to the economy's capital/output ratio. Both theories and models did not work effectively for the developing countries because more savings and investments are not sufficient for economic growth. Favorable institutional and attitudinal conditions need to be present before takeoff can take place. Michael Todaro argues the case as follows:

The Marshall plan worked for Europe because the European countries receiving aid possessed the necessary structural, institutional, and attitudinal conditions (e.g., well-integrated commodity and money markets, highly developed transport facilities, well-trained and educated manpower, the motivation to succeed, an efficient government bureaucracy) to convert new capital effectively into higher levels of output. The Rostow-Harrow-Domar models implicitly assume the existence of the same attitudes and arrangements in underdeveloped nations. Yet in many cases they are lacking, as are complementary factors such as managerial competence, skilled labor, and the ability to plan and administer a wide assortment of development projects.[67]

2. The neoclassical structural change model relies on neoclassical price and resource allocation theory and statistical modeling to describe the structural changes in the developing nations on their way to becoming modern nations. For example, the *two-sector labor theoretical model* of W. Arthur Lewis argues for a labor transfer from a traditional, overpopulated rural subsistence sector to a more productive modern urban industrial sector, and a growth of output and employment in the industrial sector.[68] Another example is the *patterns of development* empirical analysis of Hollis Chenery that identified a shift from agricultural production to industrial production as per capita income rises.[69]

3. Two streams of thought characterize the international dependency models, namely, the neoclassical dependence model and the false paradigm model.

The *neoclassical dependence model* views the world as being dominated by rich countries (the core) at the expense of poor countries (the periphery). In addition, the policies of the core countries have an effect on the peripheral countries, because of this dependency situation, and most of the time are responsible for the continuing and worsening poverty of their developing nations. The effects are perceived to be negative most of the time given the developed countries' power to control world commodities to their advantages, to dominate the domestic countries through direct foreign investment, to affect the developing economies' trade by exporting unsuitable products, and by dumping cheap products and locking them into exporting primary products with declining revenues. These accusations are well contained in the following observation:

The very forces which are set in motion by the rapid growth of rich countries—specially the development of even more sophisticated, costly and capital-incentive technologies, and of mortality-reducing health improvements and disease controls—specially a population explosion, rising unemployment and inability to develop their own technological capacities, which may in fact assume that they will not have the time needed for the continued maintenance of current growth rates, let alone their acceleration, so as to result in acceptable levels of development.[70]

A general list of the forces of international dominance and dependence is provided by Todaro.[71]

Immanuel Wallerstein argued forcefully that the core-periphery schema is fundamental, and that the exploited peripheral countries are vital to the functioning of the core countries.[72] Nations, of course, move with development from a peripheral status to either a semicore or core status.

The *false paradigm model* blames the underdevelopment of some of the developing countries on the wrong advice given by well-intentioned advisers sent to help the developing world. These experts resort to sophisticated models, some theoretical and some analytical, that are most of the time inappropriate to resolve the practical problems of underdevelopment.[73]

Domestic Problems and Policies

There are a number of critical domestic problems that are the main target of development policies in the Third World. In what follows, these problems are described and the economic policies used for their ultimate resolution are explored.

Growth, Poverty, and Income Distribution

The first problem is one of growth, poverty, and income distribution. In effect, one main objective of development is to eliminate poverty and income inequalities. As in some developed economies, the developing economies face the situation where only a small portion of the population constituting the rich class controls a very large share of the national income and resources, influencing the controls of a very large share of the national income and resources, influencing the consumption and production patterns toward expensive consumer goods. These income inequalities are aggravated by high levels of "absolute poverty," which is generally measured by the number of people living below a specified minimum level of income. Absolute poverty in the world is widespread, leading World Bank economists M. S. Ahluwalia, N. Carter, and H. Chenery to conclude that

almost 40 percent of the population of the developing countries live in absolute poverty defined in terms of income levels that are sufficient to provide adequate nutrition. The bulk of the poor are in the poorer countries: in South Asia, Indonesia and Sub-Saharian Africa. These countries account for two-thirds of the total (world) population and well over three-fourths of the population in poverty. The incidence of poverty is 60 percent or more in countries having the lowest level of real GNP.[74]

Development goals originally focused on maximizing rates of GNP growth and expecting a "trickle down" of the benefits of economic growth to the very poor. Failure of these policies led to a redefining of development goals toward broad-based income growth, with special emphasis on accelerating the growth of incomes of "target" poverty groups. Four policy options are generally advocated in determining a developing economy's distribution of income: (1) to alter the functional distribution of income through policies designed to change relative factor prices, (2) to modify the size distribution through progressive redistribution of asset ownership, (3) to reduce the size distribution at the upper levels through progressive income and wealth taxes, and (4) to affect distribution at the lower level through direct transfer payments and the public provision of goods and services.[75]

Unemployment

The second domestic problem is that of unemployment. Not only is a very large section of the population unemployed, but unemployment in the developing countries seems to grow faster than employment, mainly due to the phenomenon of labor underutilization. Edgar Edwards distinguishes among the following forms of underutilization of labor: open unemployment; underemployment; the visible active but underutilized as disguised underemployment, hidden unemployment, and prematurely retired; the impaired; and the unproductive.[76] All major economic models of employment determination are advocated in the literature, namely, classical, Keynesian, the output/employment macromodel, the price-incentive micromodel, and the two-sector labor transfer model. The classical model relies on the forces of supply and demand to set the wage rate and the level of employment. The Keynesian model relies on demand factors such as increases in government expenditures and encouragement of private investments for reducing unemployment. Both the classical and the Keynesian models are considered to be far from relevant to the developing countries. The output/employment macromodel argues that the rate of national output and employment depend on the rate of savings and investment, lending credence to the "big push" for industrialization in some developing countries. The price-incentive model maintains that the combination of labor and capital will be dictated by the relative factor prices. Cheap labor would lead to labor-intensive production processes. Finally, the two-sector labor transfer of rural-urban migration focuses on the determinants of both demand and supply. Two variations characterize the last model: the Lewis theory of development[77] and the Todaro model.[78] The Lewis model divides the economy in two sectors: (1) a traditional, rural subsistence sector characterized by zero- or low-productivity surplus labor and (2) a growing urban industrial sector characterized by an influx of labor from the subsistence sector. The Todaro model hypothesizes that migration is due to urban-rural differences in expected rather than actual earnings. All these approaches lead to a consensus position on employment strategy, which would include the following five elements: (1) creating an appropriate rural-urban economic balance; (2) expanding small-scale, labor-intensive industries; (3) eliminating factor-price distortions; (4) choosing appropriate labor-intensive technologies of production; and (5) noting the direct linkage between education and employment.[79]

Another way of reducing unemployment is by creating special zones, which are usually intended to attract foreign investors to produce assembly goods for export. The zones are made attractive to investors through offering inducements such as reducing taxes or offering tax holidays, relaxing tariffs and currency-exchange facilities, and allowing administrative advantages, which may include a watering down of union and labor laws.[80] Some groups, however, criticize the concept of special trading zones as merely sweatshops exported by "footloose" multinational companies. For example, the International Confederation of Free Trade Unions, which is the largest organization of democratic labor unions, is concerned by the possible exploitation of workers who are often desperate for jobs, and by the possible isolation of worldwide conventions on labor norms and employee protection drafted under the auspices of the UN International Labor Organization (ILO) in Geneva and ratified by most governments.

Population Growth

The third domestic problem is that of ever-expanding human numbers. All positions on the population debate seem to agree that in the long run, "zero population growth" is not only a necessity but also an important means to a better life in the developing countries. The population growth in the developing countries is now accentuated by lower death rates due undoubtedly to the rapid improvement in health conditions. As a result, one may notice that high birth rates are generally associated with national poverty and low per capita income. The question is whether population is a real problem; and whatever the position is on this question, the problem is to find adequate solutions to the population growth. Two extreme positions can be explored. The first claims that population growth is not a real problem but a result of other problems such as underdevelopment, depletion of world resources, and population distribution. The solution advocated is through development programs focusing on improvements in health, nutrition, income, social justice, status of women, and other such general factors. The second position claims that population growth is a real problem requiring deliberate governmental "population policies," which may include providing family-planning services, programs and laws affecting information and education, incentives directed toward fertility behavior, and programs to alter the frequency and age of marital unions.

Advocates of the first position attribute the decline in fertility in some developing countries to their experienced economic development, industrialization, and urbanization, while advocates of the second position point to the intensive population and family-planning programs in these countries for a better explanation of the declining birth rates. One way of solving the debate between these positions is to reach a consensus position based on a population program plus a development position.

Education

The fourth domestic problem pertains to the need for improving the human resources of the developing countries by providing a sound education system. The general mechanism used is the formal education system, which takes place in schools, uses the traditional academic curriculum, and prepares students to join modern economic lifestyles. There are, however, other types of education most beneficial to the developing countries—namely, "*informal education* or learning by doing, which includes agricultural training, programmes, evening adult literacy classes, radio and mass media campaigns, and vocational training programmes,"[81] and "*education for self-reliance* or problem-posing education, which "teaches groups of people to study together and become more aware of the political and economic determinants of their poverty.''[82]

Given the inadequacy of formal education, various developing countries have experimented with informal education and education for self-reliance. Because the results are far from conclusive at this time, the call for education reform beyond the boundaries of formal education continues to stir interest and debate in the developing countries. Education is considered to be the best determinant and hope for a better lifestyle in the developing countries. As stated by Torsten Husen, ''the mood has swung from the almost euphonic conception of education as the Great Equalizer to that of education as the Great Sieve that sorts and certifies people for their (predetermined) slot in society.''[83] Most calls for education reform stress the need for a curriculum most beneficial and in accordance with the real needs of each developing country, and more relevant to the development needs.

Agricultural Transformation and Rural Development

The fifth problem pertains to the need for agricultural transformation and rural development. One of the most proven theses in economics relates to the secular decline of the agricultural population and the labor force and agriculture's share of GNP in the course of economic development coupled with a consistent rise in the share of labor in the service sector. Various explanations are given for this structural transformation.

To some, this structural transformation is simply a consequence of development—of the increase in productivity and incomes in the various sectors of an economy that entails changes in the patterns of consumer demand and the composition of output. Other writers take the position that structural transformation should be viewed not merely as a consequence of development but as a process that should be deliberately fostered by policy measures to accelerate development and to ensure that low income, pre-industrial societies will succeed in realizing their goals of achieving self-sustained economic growth.[84]

In addition to this structural transformation, the performance of Third-World agriculture has been relatively poor due mainly to inefficiency and low productivity. Subsistence agriculture on small plots of land and extensive cultivation characterize agriculture in most of the developing countries. These countries need to move from an objective of achieving subsistence to one of agriculture sufficiency. Three stages may be necessary: a first stage of subsistence farming characterized by risk, uncertainty, and survival; a second stage of transition to mixed and diversified farming; and a third stage of specialization and modern commercial farming. To achieve this goal, a strategy of agriculture and rural development is needed. Todaro proposes three necessary conditions for rural development—land reform, supportive policies, and integrated development objectives:

Proposition I: Farm structure and land-tenure patterns need to be adopted to the dual objectives of increasing food production and promoting a wider distribution of the benefits of agrarian progress.

Proposition II: The full benefits of small-scale agricultural development cannot be realized unless government support systems are created that provide the necessary incentives, economic opportunities, and access to needed inputs to enable small cultivators to expand their output and raise their productivity.

Proposition III: Rural development, while dependent primarily on small-farmer agricultural progress, implies much more. It encompasses (a) improvements in "levels of living" including income, employment, education, health and nutrition, housing, and a variety of related social services; (b) a decreasing inequality in the distribution of rural incomes and in urban-rural imbalances on incomes and economic opportunities; and (c) the capacity of the rural sector to sustain and accelerate the pace of these improvements over time.[85]

International Problems and Policies

There are a number of critical international problems that are also the main target of development policies in the developing countries. In what follows, these problems are described and the economic policies used for their ultimate resolution are explored.[86]

International Trade and Development

Developing countries suffer from two main limitations in their trading with developed countries. First, their exports are heavily composed of nonnumerical primary products, while their imports include everything from new materials to capital goods, intermediate producer goods, and consumer products. Second, the commodity terms of trade as measured by the ratio between the price of a typical unit of exports and the price of a typical unit of imports are deteriorating. The result shows up in a continuous deficit in the current and capital accounts of their balance of payments. To solve this problem, a variety of options are used: export promotion or import-substitution policies; encouragement of private foreign investment, or call for public and private foreign assistance; greater use of the Special Drawing Rights of the International Monetary Fund (IMF); foreign exchange controls or currency devaluation; economic integration with other developing countries in the form of customs unions, free-trade areas, or common markets.[87] But above all, the major option is the choice of a trade strategy for development. Should it be an outward- or inward-looking policy? An outward-looking policy results from the classical trade theory and comparative cost-advantage arguments with the implication that free trade will maximize global output by allowing every country to specialize in what it does best. P. P. Streeten states that point as follows: "Outward-looking policies encourage not only free trade but also the free movement of capital, workers, enterprises and students, a welcome to the multinational enterprise, and open system of communications. If it does not imply laissez-faire, it certainly implies *laissez-passer*."[88]

An inward-looking policy results from the belief that the developing countries should be encouraged to engage in their own style of development and not be constrained by or dependent upon foreign importation, and to learn by doing. Streeten explains this option as follows:

Inward-looking policies emphasize the need for an indigenous technology, appropriate for the factors available in the country, and for an appropriate range of products. If you restrict trade, the movement of people and communications, if you keep out the multinational enterprise, with its wrong technology, you will evolve your own style of development and you will be stronger, more independent, master of your own fate.[89]

In short, outward-looking is identifiable with export promotion while inward-looking is identifiable with import substitution. These two strategies, when added to the strategies of primary and secondary, or manufacturing, production, yield a fourfold division: primary outward-looking policies, secondary outward-looking policies, primary inward-looking policies, and secondary inward-looking policies.[90] The choice of any one of these options determines the nature of international trade of each developing country and of its impact on development.

Foreign Investment and Aid

Many developing countries tend to rely on outside financial aid to alleviate the deficits in their current account balances. This aid takes place in the form of either private foreign investment or public development assistance. Both types of aid are examined next.

Private foreign investment is playing a major role in economic development through the activities of the large multinational corporations, whose roles are claimed to be either positive or negative, depending upon which side of the controversy one is on. Adolf Enthoven has successfully summarized the results, both positive and negative, claimed for multinational corporations by the spokespersons for developing countries as follows:

POSITIVE EFFECTS (Benefits/Advantages): 1. Transfer of capital; 2. transfer of know-how and management; 3. balance-of-payments benefits; 4. increase in competition and lower prices; 5. increase in entre-preneurial spirit; 6. help in training and education; 7. increase in employment; 8. help in infrastructure; 9. improvement of living conditions in developing countries; 10. identification, allocation, man-agement, and effective use of world material and human and financial resources; 11. greater international unity and interdependency; 12. en-suring a more equal distribution of income and wealth.

NEGATIVE EFFECTS (Costs/Disadvantages): 1. Hampering of bal-ance of payments; export of profits and interest beyond investment; 2. technology too advanced for country and too capital-intensive; 3. lim-ited training and education; 4. input of foreign management to the ne-glect of local managers; 5. curbing of local enterprises; 6. enforcement of consumption functions (luxury items); 7. uneven distribution of in-come; 8. affecting employment; restricting transfer of know-how; 9. subordination of companies and countries to the multinational corpo-rations, threatening the sovereignty of the nation-state; 10. hampering of the endogenous socioeconomic development of a nation; 11. distri-bution of social, political, and cultural patterns in the host country; 12. resentment against foreign penetration, resulting in upsetting the social balance; 13. recession resulting from inability of national industries to compete; 14. loss of national pride and nationalist spirit.[91]

Public development assistance is as much the subject of a heated debate as private foreign investment. It is viewed by some as essential and beneficial to economic development by supple-menting scarce resources and helping the developing countries to achieve more forms of self-sustaining economic growth. Oth-ers maintain that foreign aid may have retarded growth through reduced savings and worsened income inequalities.[92] They would even add that countries have strong strategic, political, and ec-onomic motivation behind their foreign aid programs. Witness the following statement made by a former U.S. aid official:

The biggest single misconception about the foreign aid programs is that we send money abroad. We don't. Foreign aid consists of American equipment, raw materials, expert services, and food—all provided for specific development projects which we ourselves review and approve. . . . Ninety-three percent of AID [Agency for International Development] funds are spent directly in the United States to pay for these things. Just last year some 4,000 American firms received $1.3 billion in AID for products supplied as part of the foreign aid program.[93]

Obviously, a new view of private foreign investments and foreign aid is needed to relieve the "disillusionment" on the part of developing countries and "weariness" on the part of developed countries. Some useful suggestions have been made in what is known as the "New International Economic Order" proposal.

New International Economic Order

Faced with their bleak situation, the developing countries began asking for a "New International Economic Order" (NIEO). In fact, the UN General Assembly, in a special session convened in April 1974 following the petroleum crisis, concluded its deliberations by committing itself to work urgently for the establishment of a new international economic order based on equity, sovereign equality, common interest, and cooperation among all states, irrespective of their economic and social systems, which would correct inequalities and redress in existing injustices, make it possible to eliminate the widening gap between the developed and the developing countries, and ensure steadily accelerating economic and social development and peace and justice for present and future generations.

Before this declaration, the United Nations began a series of programs and targets toward achieving this NIEO. Examples include launching the first UN Development Decade, the Alliance for Progress in 1961, the Yaunde Convention in 1967, and the second UN Development Decade of the 1970s. The developing countries used their newfound political and economic leverage to demand a new structure of international economic relations and a new set of rules affecting trade, industrialization, transfer of technology, and foreign assistance. A list of NIEO demands includes the following:

1. Attaining UN Official Developing Assistance targets;
2. Providing technical assistance for developing countries;

3. Renegotiating the debts of developing countries;

4. Undertaking special measures to assist land-locked, least-developed, and island-developing countries;

5. Using disarmament funds for development;

6. Improving the terms and conditions of trade for developing countries: tariff and nontariff barriers, general systems of preference, duties and taxes on imports, and invisible trade;

7. Adopting an integrated approach to commodities: the integrated program, buffer stocks, producers' associations, and indexation;

8. Developing an international food program;

9. Adjusting the economic policies of developed countries to facilitate expanding and diversifying the exports of developing countries;

10. Improving and intensifying trade relations between countries having different social and economic systems;

11. Strengthening economic and technical cooperation among developing countries;

12. Reforming the international monetary system: using special drawing rights for development assistance and as the central reserve asset of the international monetary system, promoting stable rates of exchange, and protection from the effects of inflation;

13. Assuring adequate participation by developing countries in the World Bank and IMF decision making;

14. Increasing the transfer of resources through the World Bank and the IMF;

15. Negotiating the redeployment of industrial productive capacities to developing countries;

16. Regulating and supervising the activities of transnational enterprises and eliminating restrictive business practices;

17. Improving the competitiveness of natural resources and ending their waste;

18. Providing equitable access to the resources of the seabed and the ocean floor;

19. Achieving a more equitable distribution of income and raising the level of employment;

20. Providing health services, education, higher cultural standards, and qualification for the workforce, and assuring the well-being of children and the integration of women in development;

21. Assuring the economic sovereignty of states: natural resources, foreign property, and choice of economic systems;

22. Compensating for adverse effects on the resources of states, territories, and people of foreign occupation, alien and colonial domination, or apartheid;

23. Establishing a system of consultations at global, regional, and sectoral levels with the aim of promoting industrial development; and

24. Restructuring the economic and social sections of the United Nations.[94]

The Process of Development

The process of development entails a process of economic growth expressed in terms of its components of capital accumulation, growth in population, and technological progress. It is best expressed by Simon Kuznets: "A country's economic growth may be defined as a long-term rise in capacity to supply increasingly diverse economic goods to its population, this growing capacity based on advance technology and the institutional and ideological demands that it demands."[95]

In fact, Kuznets presents six characteristics of modern economic growth in each developed country based on the conventional measures:

1. High rates of growth of per capita product and of population;

2. High rates of rise in productivity of all inputs, including labor;

3. High rates of structural transformation of the economy away from agriculture to nonagricultural pursuits, away from industry to services, and away from personal enterprise to impersonal enterprise;

4. High rates of social and ideological change, including urbanization and secularization as the components of the process of modernization;

5. Higher access of the developing countries to the markets and raw
   materials in the rest of the world; and

6. The limited spread of economic growth to only a third of the world's
   population.[96]

These characteristics are significantly interrelated. It is expressed
by Kuznets as follows:

With the rather stable ratio of labor force to total population, a high
rate of increase in per capita product means a high rate of increase in
product per worker; and, with average hours of work declining, it
means still higher growth rates in product per man-hour. Even if we
allow for the impressive accumulation of capital, in its widest sense,
the growth rate of productivity is high, and indeed, mirrors the great
rise in per capita pure consumption. Since the latter reflects the realized
effects of advancing technology, rapid changes in production structure
are inevitable—given the differential impact of technological innovations on the several production sectors, the differing income elasticity
of domestic demand for various consumer goods, and the changing
comparative advantage of foreign trade. As already indicated, advancing technology changes the scale of production plants and the character
of the economic enterprise units. Consequently, effective participation
in the modern economic system by the labor forces necessitates rapid
changes in its location and structure, in the relations among the occu-
pational status groups, and even in the relations between labor force
and total population (the last, however, within narrow overall limits).
Thus, not only are high aggregate growth rates associated with rapid
changes in economic structure, but the latter are also associated with
rapid changes in other aspects of society—in family formation, in urbanization, in man's views on his role and the measure of his achievement in society.[97]

The interdependence of growth characteristics signals to developing countries the need for a multidimensional approach to development with a stable, but flexible, political and social
framework that can accommodate the fundamental societal
changes generated by development; a positive attitude toward the

role of technological innovations and research for development; and a just relationship with rich nations that minimizes dependence and maximizes self-reliance and equity. In addition, the developing countries need to be sensitive to the emerging economic global issues that may hinder their development. One first issue is the global interdependence that places the developing countries in a situation of dependence on the rich countries, especially on four key issues: energy and resource balances, the global food-population equation, the crisis of the developing countries' debt, and the demand for a restructuring of the international economic order. Each of these issues places the destiny of the developing countries and the success of their development strategies at the doorsteps of the key developing nations. The cooperation of the developing countries becomes a key element for the success of the development of poor countries.

THE SPECIAL SITUATION OF CAPITALISM

The faces of capitalism are changing. One can distinguish four types of capitalism as follows:[98]

1. *Consumer capitalism*, as practiced in the United States, Britain, Canada, and Australia, as characterized by greater laissez-faire, open borders, small government and profit mentality, and potentially leading to problems as income in equality, low saving rates, and weak central government.

2. *Producer capitalism*, as practiced in Germany, France, Japan, and Mexico, as characterized by a focus on production, employment and statist policies, and potentially leading to problems as fraying of social safety net, showing of innovation, and consumer dissatisfaction.

3. *Family capitalism*, as practiced in Taiwan, Malaysia, Thailand, and Indonesia, and created by the Chinese diaspora, as characterized by extended clans dominating business, and by capital flows, and potentially leading to social resentment from other non-Chinese ethnics.

4. *Frontier capitalism*, as practiced by China and Russia, as

characterized by government's support for profit business activities and by the sprouting of an entrepreneurial class, and potentially leading to a rise in criminal activity. In fact, there are three stages to frontier capitalism as follows:

Stage One: Statist economies collapse or fade away. Black marketeers profit enormously, with some becoming gangsters. Government corruption spreads.

Stage Two: Small-scale entrepreneurs, often financed by family loans, flourish. Rule of law remains weak, but businesspeople start evolving their own rules of commerce.

Stage Three: Economic growth is brisk but hard to measure. Financial markets begin to evolve, tapping savings, and attracting foreign institutional investors. Clearer legal code appears.[99]

Capitalism itself may be saving a crisis as illustrated by the following theses:

A. One thesis is that the capitalist system will not cope with twenty-first-century pressures. Lester C. Thurow's evaluation of capitalism's current dilemma arises from both (a) *punctuated equilibrium* and (b) *plate tectonics*.[100] Punctuated equilibrium as the occasional suddenness of biological evolution is used to mean that winners can become sometimes quickly losers. Plate tectonics, the invisible slow movements of the continental plates floating on the earth's core, is used to mean that the causes of events may be difficult to determine and long lasting. Five economic events are presented:

1. The collapse of communism creating a vast supply of cheap and educated labor;

2. The primacy of technology creating a knowledge-based economy;

3. The demographic issue of an aging population is the rich North facing a tide of immigration from the poor South;

4. The growth of the global economy and the consequent decline in wages; and

5. The disappearance of a single globally dominant power.

Each of these events is producing changes that threaten capitalism.

B. One thesis is that nations go through periods of rise and decline, providing a case for successive primacies. Kindleberger advances the thesis in two books: *Manias, Panics, and Crashes: A History of Financial Crises*[101] and *World Economic Primacy: 1500–1900.*[102] The thesis is very much in line with a Spanish professor of jurisprudence who asserted in 1799 that: "All nations of the world, following the steps of nature, have been weak in their infancy, ignorant in their puberty, warlike in their youth, philosophic in their manhood, legists in their old age and superstitious and tyrannical in their decreptitude." It is also much in line with a *"law of interrupted progress,"* which holds that any country pioneering a new, more highly developed phase of civilization reaches a threshhold or barrier beyond which it is extremely difficult to proceed, with the result that the next step forward in the progress of mankind has to be made in another part of the world. Examples of nations following the cycle of eventual declines include:

a. The Italian city states of Venice, Florence, Geneva, and Milan;

b. Portugal and Spain following the prosperity of the fifteenth and sixteenth centuries; and

c. France, Britain, Germany, the United States, and Japan's recent histories of economic wealth turning into rigidity and resistance to change. Kindelberger cites the decline of *teamplay*, the *polarization of races and classes*, and the *shattering of American confidence following the Vietnam War* as the reasons why that nation seems to be going in the direction of sclerosis and decline.

According to the U.S. model thesis, as advocated by Francis Fukuyama,[103] it is the "end of history" with the universal triumph of American-style liberal democracy as the final form of government. The end result is not very reassuring. As stated by Fukuyama:

The end of history will be a very sad time. The struggle for recognition, the willingness to risk one's life for a purely abstract goal, the world-wide ideological struggle that called forth daring, courage, imagination, and idealism, will be replaced by economic calculation, the endless solving of technical problems, environmental concerns, and the satisfaction of sophisticated consumer demands. In the post-historical period there will be neither art nor philosophy, just the perpetual caretaking of the museum of human history. I can feel in myself, and see in others around me, a powerful nostalgia for the time when history existed. Such nostalgia, in fact, will continue to fuel competition and conflict even in the post-historical world for some time to come. Even though I recognize its inevitability, I have the most ambivalent feelings for the civilization that has been created in Europe since 1945, with its north Atlantic and Asian offshoots. Perhaps this very prospect of centuries of boredom at the end of history will serve to get history started once again.[104]

The second thesis argues that the course of events did not work according to the "end of history" scenario. According to the clash of culture hypothesis, as enunciated by Samuel P. Huntington,[105] the two blocs created by the Cold War, split into "civilizations" based on consumer cultures and heritages, are more likely to fight each other than unite in a single world based on one culture. The seven civilizations are:

a. The Western, led by the United States and Western Europe;

b. The Sinic, led by China;

c. The Hindi, led by India;

d. The Islamic, with no real leader;

e. Japan, a self-contained civilization;

f. The Orthodox, led by Russia; and

g. The African and later American civilizations, with no clear leaders.

Basically in economics and politics, there are no universal values.

C. One thesis argues for the rise of big emerging markets. The United States used to worry about economic competition from abroad by focusing on advanced industrialized democracies like Japan and Germany. A new era for the world economy dictates otherwise. The big emergent market hypothesis, or the big 10 hypothesis, as advanced by Jeffrey E. Garten,[106] stipulates that the main agents of change are a group of 10 countries that are important enough to affect the entire world economy. These countries are Argentina, Brazil, China, India, Indonesia, Mexico, Poland, South Africa, South Korea, and Turkey. They are potentially wealthy enough to play a major role in the entire world economy, providing producers everywhere with large new markets and opportunities for profit and job creation. They are in agreement with the United States in the adoption of free-market practices, while in disagreement with the United States in the role of governmental policies in influencing trade and investment flows, the rights of workers and consumers, and environmental policies.

Do these 10 countries provide a threat to the dominance of the United States or do they need American technology, American capital, and an American market that represents fully 95 percent of the world economy? This is a hypothesis that will be used for verification in the years to come.

CONCLUSIONS

For a good assessment of political risk, managers of multinational corporations need to have a thorough appreciation of the overall environment of international business and the factors most conducive to a rise in political risk. Accordingly, this chapter elaborated on (a) the special environmental factors proper to the emerging global economy, (b) the specific factors of importance to assessing the political environment, and (c) the special situation of the developing world and of capitalism. Each of these characteristics presents managers with a better perspective of the potential conditions conducive to political risk.

NOTES

1. Sak Onkvisit and John J. Shaw, *International Marketing: Analysis and Strategy*, 3rd ed. (Englewood Cliffs, NJ: Prentice-Hall, 1997), p. 142.

2. Franklin Root, *Foreign Market Entry Strategies* (New York: AMACOM, 1982), p. 146.

3. M. Porter, *The Competitive Advantage of Nations* (New York: Free Press, 1989), pp. 98–110.

4. Gerhard G. Mueller, "Whys and Hows of International Accounting," *The Accounting Review* (April 1965), p. 386.

5. J. Fred Weston and Bart W. Sorge, *International Managerial Finance* (Homewood, IL: Richard D. Irwin, 1972), p. 249.

6. David M. Raddock, *Assessing Corporate Political Risk: A Guide for International Businessmen* (Totowa, NJ: Rowman and Littlefield, 1986), pp. 6–34.

7. Ibid., p. 3.

8. C. Baldwin, "The Capital Factor: Competing for Capital in a Global Environment," in *Competition in Global Industries*, ed. M. Porter (Boston: Harvard Business School Press, 1986), pp. 184–223.

9. S. J. Gray, J. C. Shaw, and B. McSweeney, "Accounting Standards for Multinational Corporations," *Journal of International Business Studies* (Spring/Summer 1981), p. 127.

10. J. D. Daniels and L. H. Radebaugh, *International Business: Environments and Operations* (Reading, MA: Addison-Wesley, 1989).

11. J. C. Miller and B. Pras, "The Effect of Multinational and Export Diversification on the Profit Stability of US Corporations," *Southern Economic Journal* 3 (1980), pp. 78–79.

12. Raddock, *Assessing Corporate Political Risk*, pp. 6–34.

13. Onkvisit and Shaw, *International Marketing*, pp. 144–145.

14. Wroe Alderson, *Dynamic Marketing Behavior* (Homewood, IL: Richard D. Irwin, 1965).

15. Sak Onkvisit and John J. Shaw, "Myopic Management: The Hollow Strength of American Competitiveness," *Business Horizons* (January–February 1991), pp. 13–19.

16. Lyman Tower Sargent, *Contemporary Political Ideologies: A Comparative Analysis*, 9th ed. (Belmont, CA: Wadsworth, 1993), p. 3.

17. G. M. Scott, *Political Science: Foundations for a Fifth Millennium* (Englewood Cliffs, NJ: Prentice-Hall, 1997), p. 81.

18. E. Burke, "Reflections on the Revolution in France," in E. Burke, *Reflections on the Revolution in France and the Rights of Man* (Garden City, NY: Dolphin Books, 1992).

19. George Gilder, *Wealth and Poverty* (New York: Basic Books, 1981).

20. Irving Kristol, "Confessions of a True, Self-Confessed—Perhaps the Only—'Neoconservative,' " *Public Opinion* (October/November 1979), p. 171.

21. Scott, *Political Science*, p. 92.

22. Thomas L. Brewer, "Political Risk Assessment for Foreign Direct Investment Decisions: Better Methods for Better Results," *Columbia Journal of World Business* (Spring 1981), pp. 5–12.

23. Thomas L. Brewer, *American Foreign Policy: A Contemporary Introduction* (Englewood Cliffs, NJ: Prentice-Hall, 1980).

24. Ibid., p. 52.

25. Ibid., p. 43.

26. Brewer, "Political Risk Assessment for Foreign Direct Investment Decisions," p. 6.

27. G. T. Allison, *Essence of a Decision: Explaining the Cuban Missile Crisis* (Boston: Little, Brown, 1971).

28. Ibid., p. 31.

29. Ibid.

30. J. D. Cheshire and E. H. Feroz, "Allison's Models, and the FASB Statements Nos. 2, 5, 13, and 19," *Journal of Business Finance and Accounting* (Spring 1989), p. 120.

31. Robert Axelrod, *Framework for a General Theory of Cognition and Choice* (Berkeley, CA: Institute of International Studies, 1972).

32. Ibid., p. 51.

33. Chong-Do Hah and Robert M. Lindquist, "The 1952 Steel Seizure Revisited: A Systematic Study in Presidential Decision Making," *Administrative Science Quarterly* (December 1975), pp. 587–605.

34. Ibid., p. 602.

35. Gabriel Almond, *A Discipline Divided: Schools and Sects in Political Science* (Newbury Park, CA: Sage, 1990).

36. Diana Coole, "Feminism and Politics," in *New Developments in Political Science: An International Review of Achievements and Prospects*, ed. A. Leftwich (Brookfield, VT: Edward Elgar Publishing, 1990).

37. James David Barber, *The Presidential Character: Predicting Performance in the White House* (Englewood Cliffs, NJ: Prentice-Hall, 1972).

38. Allison, *Essence of a Decision*.

39. James M. Buchanan and Robert D. Tollison, *Theory of Public Choice* (Ann Arbor: University of Michigan Press, 1972).

40. Peter C. Ordershook, "The Development of Contemporary Political Theory," in *Political Economy: Institutions, Competition and Representation*, ed. W. A. Barnett, R. J. Hinich, and N. J. Schofield (Cambridge: Cambridge University Press, 1993).

41. D. Easton, *Political Science in the United States: Past and Present* (London and New York: Routledge, 1991).

42. Gabriel Almond, *The Politics of Developing Areas* (Princeton, NJ: Princeton University Press, 1960).

43. Karl Deutsch, *The Nerves of Government: Models of Human Communication and Control* (New York: Free Press, 1963).

44. Roy C. Macridis, *The Study of Comparative Politics* (New York: Random House, 1955).

45. Leo Strauss, *What Is Political Philosophy?* (New York: Free Press, 1959).

46. Eric Voeglin, *The New Science of Politics* (Chicago: University of Chicago Press, 1952).

47. R. Rubinson and C. Chase-Dunn, "Cycles, Trends, and New Departures in World System Development," in *National Development and World Systems*, ed. J. W. Meyer, and M. T. Hannan (Chicago: University of Chicago Press, 1979).

48. Scott, *Political Science*, p. 164.

49. R. T. Green, "Political Structures as a Predictor of Radical Political Change," *Columbia Journal of World Business* (Spring 1974), pp. 22–36.

50. Ibid., p. 30.

51. Ibid., p. 31.

52. Ibid., p. 34.

53. Ibid., p. 34.

54. Dennis Goulet, *The Cruel Choice: A New Concept in the Theory of Development* (New York: Atheneum, 1971), p. 23.

55. Michael P. Todaro, *Economic Development in the Third World* (New York: Longman, 1985), p. 28.

56. Gunnar Myrdal, *Asian Drama* (New York: Pantheon, 1968), Appendix 2.

57. Todaro, *Economic Development*, p. 24.

58. Ibid., p. 17.

59. Myrdal, *Asian Drama*, pp. 16–17.

60. Keith Griffin and Azizur Rahman Khan, "Poverty in the Third World: Ugly Facts and Fancy Models," *World Development* 6, 3 (1978), pp. 301–302.

61. Louis Feber, "On the Paradigm for Economic Development," *World Development* 2, 1 (1974), pp. 6–7.

62. Irma Adelman, "Development Economics: A Reassessment of Goals," *American Economic Review* (May 1975), p. 306.

63. Goulet, *The Cruel Choice*, pp. 87–95.

64. Ibid., p. 88.

65. Ibid., p. 90.

66. W. W. Rostow, *The Stages of Economic Growth: A Non-Communist Manifesto* (London: Cambridge University Press, 1960).

67. Todaro, *Economic Development*, pp. 66–67.

68. W. A. Lewis, "Economic Development with Unlimited Supplies of Labor," *Manchester School*, 1954; and J. C. H. Fei and G. Ranis, *Development of the Labor Surplus Economy: Theory and Policy* (Homewood, IL: Irwin, 1964).

69. Hollis Chenery, *Structural Changes and Development Policy* (Baltimore: Johns Hopkins University Press, 1979).

70. Hans W. Singer, "Dualism Revisited: A New Approach to the Problems of Dual Society in Developing Countries," *Journal of Developmental Studies*, 7, 1 (1970), p. 40

71. Todaro, *Economic Development*, p. 80.

72. Immanuel Wallerstein, *The Capitalist World Economy* (Cambridge: Cambridge University Press, 1979), p. 73.

73. Todaro, *Economic Development*, p. 80.

74. M. S. Ahluwalia, N. Carter, and H. Chenery, "Growth and Poverty in Developing Countries," *Journal of Development Studies* 7, 1 (1970), p. 306.

75. Todaro, *Economic Development*, p. 80.

76. Edgar O. Edwards, *Employment in Developing Countries: Report on a Ford Foundation Study* (New York: Columbia University Press, 1974), pp. 10–11.

77. Lewis, "Economic Development with Unlimited Supplies of Labor." The model was formalized and extended in J. C. H. Fei and G. Ramis, "A Theory of Economic Development," *American Economic Review* 51, 3 (1961), p. 210.

78. Michael P. Todaro, "A Model of Labor Migration and Urban Unemployment in Less Developed Countries," *American Economic Review* 59, 1, (1969), pp. 138–148.

79. Todaro, *Economic Development*, pp. 244–245.

80. David Fonguet, "Special Trade Zones Increase Despite Cities," *Chicago Tribune* (November 17, 1983), sect. 2, pp. 2–3.

81. John Simmons, "Education for Development, Reconsidered," *World Development* (1979), p. 1006.

82. Ibid.

83. Torsten Husen, "Problems of Securing Equal Access to Higher Education: The Dilemma between Equality and Excellence," *Higher Education* 5 (1976), p. 411.

84. Bruce F. Jonston, "Agricultural and Structural Transformation in Developing Countries: A Survey of Research," *Journal of Economic Literature* 8, 2 (1970), p. 374.

85. Todaro, *Economic Development*, pp. 278–280.

86. Ahmed Belkaoui, *International Accounting* (Westport, CT: Quorum Books, 1985), p. 320.

87. Felipe Pazos, "Regional Integration of Trade among Less Developed Countries: A Survey of Research," *Journal of Economic Literature* 8, 2 (1970), p. 374.

88. P. P. Streeten, "Trade Strategies for Development: Some Themes for the Seventies," *World Development* 1, 6 (June 1973), p. 1.89.

89. Ibid., p. 2.

90. Ibid.

91. Adolf J. H. Enthoven, *Social and Political Impact of Multinationals on Third World Countries (and its Accounting Implications)* (Dallas: Center for International Accounting Development, The University of Texas at Dallas, 1976), p. 2.

92. K. Griffin and J. L. Enos, "Foreign Assistance: Objectives and

Consequences,'' *Economic Development and Cultural Change* (April 1970), pp. 313–327.

93. W. S. Gand, ''Foreign Aid: What Is It, How It Works, Why We Provide It,'' *Department of State Bulletin* 59, 1537 (1968), p. 50.

94. A thorough description of each of these demands and the history of its organization is provided in E. Laszlo, R. Basler, Jr., E. Eisenberg, and V. Raman, *The Objectives of the New International Economic Order* (New York: Pergamon Press, 1978).

95. Simon Kuznets, ''Modern Economic Growth: Findings and Reflections,'' *American Economic Review* (June 1973), pp. 248–249.

96. Ibid.

97. Ibid., p. 250.

98. Christopher Farrell, ''The Triple Revolution,'' *Business Week*, Special 1994 Bonus Issue, p. 19.

99. K. Pennar, P. Galuszka, and K. L. Miller, ''Capitalism in Transition,''*Business Week*, Special 1994 Bonus Issue, p. 28.

100. Lester C. Thurow, *The Future of Capitalism: How Today's Economic Forces Shape Tomorrow's World* (New York: William Morrow and Company, 1996).

101. Charles P. Kindleberger, *Manias, Panics and Crashes: A History of Financial Crises* (New York: John Wiley, 1996).

102. Charles P. Kindleberger, *World Economic Primacy: 1500–1900* (Oxford: Oxford University Press, 1996).

103. Francis Fukáyama, ''The End of History?'' *The National Interest* (Summer 1989), pp. 3–18.

104. Ibid., p. 18.

105. Samuel P. Huntington, ''The Clash of Civilizations and the Remaking of the World Order,'' *Foreign Affairs* 2 (1977), p. 30.

106. Jeffrey E. Garten, *The Big Ten* (New York: Basic Books, 1997).

SELECTED READINGS

Allison, Graham. *Essence of a Decision: Explaining the Cuban Missile Crisis.* Boston: Little, Brown, 1971.

Brewer, Thomas. L. *American Foreign Policy: A Contemporary Introduction.* Englewood Cliffs, NJ: Prince-Hall, 1980.

Porter, M. *The Competitive Advantage of Nations.* New York: Free Press, 1989.

2

The Economic Environment

INTRODUCTION[1]

Political risk is defined by both the political and economic environments of each country. Chapter 1 presented the political environment. Separating political risk from economic risk has been denounced by Overholt who argued for the importance of political-economic integration as follows:

The division of academic curricula into distinct disciplines creates the false illusion that politics can be separated from economics. It is possible for an economist to obtain a doctorate in economics without having studied politics, and vice versa for political scientists. In fact, most of politics is a struggle over economic decisions. . . . Very few examples discussed . . . are narrowly political. The scenarios typically are political-economic. The businessman is interested in the economic consequences of political decisions.[2]

Accordingly, this chapter presents the economic environment of interest to political risk, namely, the determinants of economic growth. Economic growth and political risk affect each other. The question "What determines the rate of economic growth?" has been and is still the subject of research interest.[3–6]

The search is for empirical linkages between long-run average growth rates and fiscal, trade, and monetary indicators as suggested by theory.[7] The research to date has not considered the potential impact of accounting information adequacy on economic growth.

Economic research either assumes that accounting is given or that the impact of accounting is inconsequential, or both.[8] As accounting is assumed to establish the links of firms to the economy[9,10] and perform a critical function in any economy,[11-15] its inclusion in macroeconomic models of growth is warranted. Accordingly, based on a set of hypotheses, this chapter examines the cross-sectional relationship between economic growth, on one hand, and macroeconomic and accounting information adequacy variables, on the other hand. Specifically, the chapter relies on 1980–1988 data from 31 countries to construct a pooled cross-sectional data set and examines the association of five variables with economic growth. These variables are (1) gross domestic investment as a percentage of GDP, (2) annual rate of inflation, (3) terms of trade, (4) total expenditures on health and education as percentage of GDP, and (5) accounting information adequacy. The results support the significant impact of accounting information adequacy, in addition to the other four macroeconomic variables, on economic growth.

GENERAL GROWTH MODEL

The empirical growth literature has relied on the following cross-sectional specification:

$$Y = B_i I + B_m M + B_z Z + u \tag{1}$$

where Y is the per capita growth in GNP, I is a set of variables always included in the regression, M is a variable of interest, and Z is a subset of variables generally believed to be important explanatory variables of growth. The I variables are inspired by new growth models that rely on constant returns to reproducible inputs or endogenous technological change. Gross domestic investment as a percentage of GDP is used as the I variable in this study. The variable of interest, M, is accounting information adequacy. Finally, the Z variables represent fiscal, trade, and monetary indicators, as suggested by theory and earlier research. This chapter uses annual rate of inflation, terms of trade, and total expenditures on health and education as a percentage of GDP as Z variables included in the model. The next section considers a set of hypotheses that support the variables included in the model.

HYPOTHESES AND VARIABLES

The hypotheses are drawn on the basis of the following characteristics: (1) they include the impact of accounting information adequacy, (2) they rely on macroeconomic rationales, (3) they yield testable implications for economic growth, and (4) they can be supported by available data.

Gross Domestic Investment as a Percentage of GDP

Out of 41 growth studies, 33 included gross domestic investment as a percentage of GDP as an I variable. In addition, economic theory holds that higher rates of saving and investment are essential to the long-run rate of growth of a nation.[16] The intuition behind Solow's[17] framework is that higher investment over savings rates lead to more accumulated capital per worker, resulting in an increase in the per capita output of the economy, but at a decreasing rate. In endogenous growth models with an emphasis on broader concepts of capital, such as that of Rebelo,[18] per capita growth and the investment ratio tend to move together. Delong and Summers,[19] looking at a cross section of countries in the postwar period, find a positive association between investment in machinery and equipment and faster rates of growth. Based on the above empirical and theoretical evidence, this chapter relies on gross domestic investment as a percentage of GDP as a potential positive determinant of economic growth.

Annual Rate of Inflation

The Tobin-Mundell hypotheses imply that anticipated inflation causes more rapid shifts from real money balances toward real capital, raising investment, and economic growth. Conversely, Stockman[20] implied that, in economies with "cash-in-advance" constraints, anticipated inflation reduces economic activity and economic growth. Based on the above theoretical rationales, this study relies on the annual rate of inflation as a potential determinant of economic growth. A positive relationship will support the Tobin-Mundell hypotheses, while a negative relationship will support Stockman's hypothesis.

Terms of Trade

Export promotion policies have a beneficial impact on economic growth.[21] Similarly, trade restrictions are expected to have an adverse effect on the efficiency of the economy by causing the failure to exploit comparative advantage and the reduction of aggregate output.[22] One factor associated with higher exports and lower trade restrictions is the commodity or net barter terms of trade. Terms of trade is a ratio of two indices: (1) the average price of a country's exports, which are approximated by dividing an index of export volume into an index of export revenue, and (2) the average price of its imports, determined by the same method. Terms of trade is used as a determinant of economic growth. Thus, countries in which terms of trade are greater may be expected to experience greater economic growth.

Total Expenditures on Health and Education as a Percentage of GDP

The impact of government expenditures on economic growth has led to a policy debate among developmental economists.

Supply-side theorists argue that the taxes required for financing government expenditures distort incentives and reduce efficient resource allocation and the level of output.[23,24] Basically, countries with greater mean growth in governmental expenditures experience lower economic growth. The empirical growth literature uses (1) measures of overall size of the government in the economy, (2) disaggregated measures of government expenditures, and (3) measures of the growth rates of government expenditures. Disaggregated measures of government expenditures have been adopted in this chapter because of data availability. Thus, countries with greater total expenditures on health and education as a percentage total GDP should experience lower economic growth in the short run.

Accounting Information Adequacy

Accounting is assumed to be an important positive determinant of economic growth. This hypothesis is based on the following arguments:

1. Information produced by the accounting system serves the economy by allowing for increases in the efficiency of resource allocation among competing interests.

2. An important element of the efficient capital market is the existence of a sophisticated accounting infrastructure comprised of the facilities of information production, the framework of information monitoring, and contract enforcement.[25]

3. Accounting information disclosures stimulates economic growth through its beneficial effect on the market capital accumulation.[26]

4. Accounting information is vital to the planning, decision-making, performance evaluation, and data-structuring processes of various economic institutions vital to economic growth.

5. Three alternative perspectives on accounting method choice—the opportunistic behavior, efficient contracting, and information perspectives—may be relevant to the accounting information adequacy thesis.[27,28] The efficient contracting hy-

pothesis implies that accounting methods are chosen to minimize agency costs among the various parties to the firm, hence resulting in maximizing the value of the firm.[29] According to the opportunistic behavior perspective, the same choice allows managers to behave opportunistically to transfer wealth. Finally, the information perspective implies that the accounting methods are selected to provide information about the future cash flows of the firm, but do not affect them directly.[30] The opportunistic behavior and efficient contracting hypotheses link accounting to cash flows and wealth transfer, implying that accounting ultimately affects economic growth. Thus, countries with higher accounting information adequacy may be expected to experience greater economic growth.

To measure accounting information adequacy, research examining the relationship between accounting and its environment has generally relied on disclosure indices based on the disclosure practices of large corporations in developed and developing countries.[31] One exception is a recent study by Adhikari and Tondkar[32] that relied on an alternative proxy, the operationalization of listing and filing requirements of stock exchanges in different countries, for measuring the general level of accounting disclosures in different countries. This level of stock exchange disclosure requirements was used in this study as the measure of accounting information adequacy and is hypothesized as a positive determinant of economic growth. Thus, countries in which the general level of disclosure required by stock exchanges is greater may be expected to experience greater economic growth.

Empirical Design

The hypotheses were tested using a two-stage regression specified as follows:

$$GNPG_j = a_0 + a_1 GDIG_j + a_2 AIA_j + a_3 ARI_j + a_4 TOT_j + \qquad (2)$$
$$a_5 TEHEG_j + u''_j$$

where

   GNPG = GNP per capita annual growth
   GDIG = Gross domestic investment as a percentage of gross
             domestic product (GDP)
     AIA = Accounting information adequacy
     ARI = The annual rate of inflation
     TOT = Terms of trade
  TEHEG = Total expenditures on health and education as a
             percentage of GDP
        j = country *j*

A two-stage regression was used because of the possibility that economic growth also causes accounting information adequacy. All the variables are measured for the 1980–1988 period. The data for this chapter come from the *Human Development Report* of the United Nations[33] and the *International Financial Statistics* of the International Monetary Fund. Accounting information adequacy is measured by the level of accounting disclosure required by stock exchanges. The 31 countries were chosen because they had available data for all the variables used in this chapter. The list of countries is shown in Exhibit 2.1.

THE EMPIRICAL RESULTS

The correlation coefficients are reported in Exhibit 2.2. There is no evidence of serious multicollinearity among all the independent variables. The RESET (regression specification error test), as suggested by Ramsey[34] and Thurby,[35,36] and the Hausman test,[37] as suggested by Wu,[38] were used as specification tests. The results of the RESET test, used to check omitted variables, incorrect functional form, and nonindependence of regressors, shows that the model used in this chapter is not misspecified (see diagnostic check statistics in Exhibit 2.3).

Exhibit 2.3 provides the results of estimating Equation (2) for the sample of 31 countries using the two-stage regression. The model explains about 57 percent of the variation in measured economic growth. The residuals appear normally distributed and

Exhibit 2.1
List of Countries

1. Australia	12. India	23. South Africa
2. Austria	13. Italy	24. Spain
3. Brazil	14. Japan	25. Sweden
4. Canada	15. Korea	26. Switzerland
5. Colombia	16. Malaysia	27. Thailand
6. Denmark	17. Mexico	28. Turkey
7. Egypt	18. Netherlands	29. United Kingdom
8. Finland	19. New Zealand	30. United States
9. France	20. Norway	31. Venezuela
10. Germany	21. Pakistan	
11. Greece	22. Singapore	

Source: A. Riahi-Belkaoui, "Accounting Information Adequacy and Macro-economic Determinants of Economic Growth: Cross-Country Evidence," *Advances in International Accounting* 8 (1995), p. 92. Reprinted with permission of JAI Press.

include no clear outliers (the standard deviation of residuals based on N-K degrees of freedom is s.d. $2 = 0.0086$). The F-statistic for the regression, $F = 6.42$, rejects the null hypotheses of no explanatory power for the regression as a whole at better than in the one percent level.

The individual coefficients on the macroeconomic variables were all significant with the expected sign: (1) positive for gross domestic investment as a percentage of GDP, as expected from the new growth models; (2) positive for terms of trade, as expected by the export promotion policy implications; (3) negative for inflation; and (4) negative for total expenditures on health and education as a percentage of GDP, as expected from the "supply-side" hypothesis. Of more relevance to this study is the significant and positive influence of accounting information adequacy, as measured by the general level accounting disclosure required by stock exchanges. A stepwise regression identified the relative importance of each of the independent variables in ex-

Exhibit 2.2
Summary Statistics and Correlation Coefficients of Independent Variables

Variables	Mean	Standard Deviation	Median	AIA	ARI	TOT	TEHEG
GDIC*	23.7	4.8	23.0	.1188 (.474)	-.1201 (.5123)	.0567 (.7577)	-.1619 (.3758)
AIA	68.8	9.6	70.6	1.000 (.555)	-.1064 (.3750)	.1595 (.0331)	.3718
ARI	16.2	33.8	7.1		1.000	.0394 (.8277)	-.3142 (.0798)
TOT	96.9	22.3	103.0			1.000	.2598 (.1509)
TEHEG	9.9	4.5	10.5				1.000
GNPG	3.0	1.6	2.7				

Notes: GDIC* = Gross Domestic Investment as a Percentage of GDP
AIA = Accounting Information Adequacy
ARI = Annual Rate of Inflation
TOT = Terms of Trade
TEHEG = Total expenditures on Health and Education as a Percentage of GDP
GNPG = Per Capita Annual Growth in GNP.

Source: A. Riahi-Belkaoui, "Accounting Information Adequacy and Macroeconomic Determinants of Economic Growth: Cross-Country Evidence," *Advances in International Accounting* 8 (1995), p. 93. Reprinted with permission of JAI Press.

plaining economic growth in the following order: (1) gross domestic investment as a percentage of GDP, (2) terms of trade, (3) annual rate of inflation, (4) total expenditures on health and education as a percentage of GDP, and (5) accounting information adequacy.

In addition, the results of the Hausman F-test show that the hypothesis of the econometric exogeneity of accounting information disclosure adequacy cannot be rejected at 0.01 level, indicating that no simultaneous equation bias was observed. More specifically, based on previous empirical studies,[39–41] the instrumental variables used in the equation specifying accounting adequacy included economic growth and the UN *Human Development Index*. This index is considered a more realistic

Exhibit 2.3
Results of the Regression Model

Variables	Intercept	GDIG	AIA	ARI	TOT	TEHEG	R^2	RESET F-value	Hausman F-value
B-value	-4.878	0.112	0.058	-0.015	0.028	-0.141			
t-ratio	-1.814**	2.641*	2.652*	-2.59*	3.065*	-2.56*	.57	0.005	6.42*

Notes: * = Significant at alpha = 0.01.
       ** = Significant at alpha = 0.10.

Source: A. Riahi-Belkaoui, ''Accounting Information Adequacy and Macro-economic Determinants of Economic Growth: Cross-Country Evidence,'' *Advances in International Accounting* 8 (1995), p. 93. Reprinted with permission of JAI Press.

measure of human development than mere GNP per head. It is included in this equation to relate disclosure adequacy to both economic and human development. The equation in the second stage of the two-stage regression was as follows:

$$AIA_j = b_0 + b_1 GNPG_j + HDI_j + u''_j \tag{3}$$

where

HDI_j = Human Development Index for country j.

The results, as shown in Exhibit 2.4, indicate that economic growth is not a significant explanator of accounting adequacy. However, *HDI* is found to be a significant explanator of accounting adequacy. Both results add more strength to the main result of this chapter, that accounting adequacy causes economic growth.

CONCLUSION

This chapter presents the results of an explanatory empirical study on the impact of macroeconomic factors and accounting disclosure adequacy on economic growth. There are two major

Exhibit 2.4
Results of the Second Regression

Variables	Intercept	GNPG	HDI	R^2	F
b value	46.090	0.821	23.530	0.81	3.727**
t-ratio	5.345*	0.622	2.655*		

Notes: * = Significant at alpha = 0.01.
         ** = Significant at alpha = 0.05.

Source: A. Riahi-Belkaoui, "Accounting Information Adequacy and Macroeconomic Determinants of Economic Growth: Cross-Country Evidence,"
   Advances in International Accounting 8 (1995), p. 94. Reprinted with permission of JAI Press.

empirical results in this chapter. First, in accordance with macroeconomic hypotheses, economic growth was found to be positively related to gross domestic investment as a percentage of
GDP and terms of trade, and negatively related to inflation rate
and total expenditure on health and education as a percentage of
GDP. Second, accounting disclosure adequacy, as measured by
the accounting disclosure requirements of the stock exchanges
of the countries included in the sample, was found to be positively related to economic growth as it provides the information
links needed for the efficient functioning of the investment, trade,
fiscal, and monetary forces in the economy. More work needs to
be done with alternative measures for all the independent variables used in this chapter as well as different periods of analysis.

NOTES

1. Parts of this chapter have been adapted with permission of the
publisher from A. Riahi-Belkaoui, "Accounting Information Adequacy
and Macroeconomic Determinants of Economic Growth: Cross-
Country Evidence," *Advances in International Accounting* 8 (1995),
pp. 87–97.
2. William H. Overholt, *Political Risk* (London: Euromoney
Publications, 1982).
3. Ibid., p. 124.

4. P. M. Romer, "Capital, Labor, and Productivity," *Brooking Papers on Economic Activity* (1990), pp. 337–420.

5. N. Stern, "The Determinants of Growth," *The Economic Journal* (January 1991), pp. 122–123.

6. R. J. Barro, "Economic Growth in a Cross Section of Countries," *Quarterly Journal of Economics* (May 1991), pp. 407–444.

7. R. Levine and D. Renelt, "A Sensitivity Analysis of Cross-Country Growth Regressions," *The American Economic Review* (September 1992), pp. 942–963.

8. J. A. Talaga and G. Ndubizu, "Accounting and Economic Development: Relationships among Paradigms," *International Journal of Accounting Education and Research* 21, 2 (1986), pp. 55–68.

9. P. Prakash and A. Rappaport, "Informational Interdependencies," *The Accounting Review* (October 1975), pp. 723–734.

10. A. Riahi-Belkaoui, *Accounting Theory*, 3rd ed. (London: Academic Press, 1992).

11. G. M. Scott, "Private Enterprise Accounting in Developing Nations," *International Journal of Accounting* 4 (1968), pp. 51–65.

12. J. B. Ghartey, *Crisis Accountability and Development in the Third World* (Aldershot, UK: Avebury, 1987).

13. A. J. H. Enthoven, *Accountancy and Economic Development Policy* (Amsterdam: North-Holland, 1973).

14. R. K. Larson, "International Accounting Standards and Economic Growth: An Empirical Investigation of their Relationship in Africa," *Research in Third World Accounting* 2 (1992), pp. 27–43.

15. A. Riahi-Belkaoui, *International and Multinational Accounting* (Fort Worth, TX: Dryden Press, 1994).

16. C. I. Plossner, "The Search for Growth," in *Policies for Long-run Economic Growth* (Kansas City: Federal Reserve Bank of Kansas, 1992), pp. 57–86.

17. R. Solow, "A Contribution to the Theory of Economic Growth," *Quarterly Journal of Economics* 70 (1956), pp. 65–94.

18. S. Rebelo, "Long-Run Policy Analysis and Long-Run Growth," *Journal of Political Economy* 99 (1991), pp. 500–521.

19. J. B. Delong and L. H. Summers, "Macroeconomic Policy and Long-Run Growth," *Policies for Long-Run Economic Growth* (Kansas City: Federal Reserve Bank of Kansas, 1992), pp. 93–128.

20. A. Stockman, "Anticipated Inflation and the Capital Stock in a

Cash-in-Advance Economy," *Journal of Monetary Economics* 8 (1981), pp. 387–393.

21. G. Feder, "On Exports and Economic Growth," *Journal of Development Economics* 12 (1982), pp. 59–73.

22. R. C. Kormendi and P. G. Meguire, "Macroeconomic Determinants of Growth: Cross-Country Evidence," *Journal of Monetary Economics* 16 (1985), pp. 141–163.

23. K. B. Grier and G. Tullock, "An Empirical Analysis of Cross-National Economic Growth, 1951–80," *Journal of Monetary Economics* 29 (1989), pp. 259–276.

24. E. F. Denison, *Trends in American Economic Growth: 1929–82* (Washington, DC: The Brookings Institution, 1985).

25. C. J. Lee, "Accounting Infrastructure and Economic Development," *Journal of Accounting and Public Policy* 6 (1987), pp. 75–85.

26. G. A. Ndubizu, "Accounting Disclosures Methods and Economic Development: A Criteria for Globalizing Capital Markets," *The International Journal of Accounting* 27 (1992), pp. 151–163.

27. R. Holthausen, "Accounting Method Choice, Opportunistic Behavior, Efficient Contracting, and Information Perspectives," *Journal of Accounting and Economics* 12 (1990), pp. 207–218.

28. P. Healey, "The Effects of Bonus Schemes on Accounting Decisions," *Journal of Accounting and Economics* 7 (1985), pp. 85–107.

29. R. Watts, "Corporate Financial Statements, a Product of the Market and Political Processes," *Australian Journal of Management* 2 (1977), pp. 53–78.

30. R. Holthausen and R. Leftwich, "The Economic Consequences of Accounting Choice: Implications of Costly Contracting and Monitoring," *Journal of Accounting and Economics* 5 (1983), pp. 77–117.

31. R. S. O. Wallace and H. Gernon, "Frameworks for International Comparative Financial Reporting," *Journal of Accounting Literature* 19 (1991), pp. 209–264.

32. A. Adhikari and R. H. Tondkar, "Environmental Factors Influencing Accounting Disclosure Requirement of Global Stock Exchanges," *Journal of International Financial Management and Accounting* 4 (1992), pp. 75–105.

33. United Nations, *Human Development Report* (New York: United Nations, 1990).

34. T. Ramsey, "Test for Specification Errors in Classical Linear

Squares Regression Analysis,'' *Journal of the Royal Statistical Society* 31, Series B (1969), p. 31.

35. J. Thursby, ''A Test for Strategy for Discriminating between Auto-Correlation and Misspecification in Regression Analysis,'' *Review of Economics and Statistics* 63 (1981), pp. 117–123.

36. J. Thursby, ''The Relationship among the Specification Test of Hausman, Ramsey and Chow,'' *Journal of Accounting and Literature* 80 (1985), pp. 926–928.

37. J. A. Hausman, ''Specification Tests in Econometrics,'' *Econometrics* (1978), pp. 1251–1270.

38. P. Wu, ''Alternative Test of Independence between Stochastic Regressors and Disturbances,'' *Econometrics* 2 (1973), pp. 733–750.

39. A. Belkaoui, ''Economic, Political and Civil Indicators and Reporting and Disclosure Adequacy: Empirical Investigation,'' *Journal of Accounting and Public Policy* (Fall 1983), pp. 207–219.

40. A. Belkaoui and M. Maksy, ''Welfare of the Common Man and Accounting Disclosure Adequacy: An Empirical Investigation,'' *The International Journal of Accounting* (Spring 1985), pp. 81–94.

41. T. E. Cook and R. S. O. Wallace, ''Financial Disclosure Refutation and Its Environment; A Review and Further Analysis,'' *Journal of Accounting and Public Policy* 9 (1990), pp. 79–110.

SELECTED READINGS

Adhikari, A., and R. H. Tondhar. ''Environmental Factors Influencing Accounting Disclosure Requirements of Global Stock Exchanges.'' *Journal of International Financial Management and Accounting* 4 (1992), pp. 75–105.

Barro, R. J. ''Economic Growth in a Cross Section of Countries.'' *Quarterly Journal of Economics* (May 1991), pp. 407–444.

Belkaoui, A. ''Economic, Political and Civil Indicators and Reporting and Disclosure Adequacy: Empirical Investigation.'' *Journal of Accounting and Public Policy* (Fall 1983), pp. 207–219.

Belkaoui, A., and M. Maksy. ''Welfare of the Common Man and Accounting Disclosure Adequacy: An Empirical Investigation.'' *The International Journal of Accounting* (Spring 1985), pp. 81–94.

Blitzen, C. R. *Economy-Wide Models and Development Planning.* London: Oxford University Press, 1975.

Bornschier, V., C. Chase-Dunn, and R. Rubinstein. "Cross-National Evidence of the Effects of Foreign Investment and Aid on Economic Growth and Inequality: A Survey of Findings and Re-Analysis." *American Journal of Sociology* 84 (1978), pp. 651–683.

Chenery, H. B., S. Robinson and M. Syrguin. *Industrialization and Growth: A Comparative Study.* London: Oxford University Press, 1986

Chenery, H. B., and T. N. Srivivasan. *Handbook of Development Economics. 2nd ed.* Amsterdam: North-Holland, 1985.

Chenery, H. B., and L. J. Taylor. "Development Patterns: Among Countries and Over Time." *Review of Economics and Statistics* (November 1968), pp. 391–416.

Cook, T. E., and R. S. O. Wallace. "Financial Disclosure Refulation and Its Environment: A Review and Further Analysis." *Journal of Accounting and Public Policy* 9 (1990), pp. 79–110.

De Gregorio, J. "The Effects of Inflation on Economic Growth." *European Economic Review* 36 (1992), pp. 417–425.

Delong, J. B., and L. H. Summers. "Macroeconomic Policy and Long-Run Growth." *Policies for Long-Run Economic Growth.* Kansas City: Federal Reserve Bank of Kansas, 1992, pp. 93–128.

Denison, E. F. *Trends in American Economic Growth: 1929–82.* Washington, DC: The Brookings Institution, 1985.

Enthoven, A. J. H. *Accountancy and Economic Development Policy.* Amsterdam: North-Holland, 1973.

Feder, G. "On Exports and Economic Growth." *Journal of Development Economics* 12 (1982), pp. 59–73.

Ghartey, J. B. *Crisis Accountability and Development in the Third World.* Aldershot, UK: Avebury, 1987.

Grier, K. B., and G. Tullock. "An Empirical Analysis of Cross-National Economic Growth, 1951–80." *Journal of Monetary Economic* 29 (1989), pp. 259–276.

Hausman, J. A. "Specification Tests in Econometrics." *Econometrics* 12 (1978), pp. 1251–1270.

Healey, P. "The Effects of Bonus Schemes on Accounting Decisions." *Journal of Accounting and Economics* 7 (1985), pp. 85–107.

Holthausen, R. "Accounting Method Choice, Opportunistic Behavior, Efficient Contracting, and Information Perspectives." *Journal of Accounting and Economics* 12 (1990), pp. 207–218.

Holthausen, R., and R. Leftwich. "The Economic Consequences of Accounting Choice: Implications of Costly Contracting and Monitoring." *Journal of Accounting and Economics* 5 (1983), pp. 77–117.

Kohn, M. L. *Cross National Research in Sociology.* Newbury Park, CA: Sage, 1989.

Kormendi, R. C., and P. G. Meguire. "Macroeconomic Determinants of Growth: Cross-Country Evidence." *Journal of Monetary Economics* 16 (1985), pp. 141–163.

Larson, R. K. "International Accounting Standards and Economic Growth: An Empirical Investigation of Their Relationship in Africa." *Research in Third World Accounting* 2 (1992), pp. 27–43.

Lee, C. J. "Accounting Infrastructure and Economic Development." *Journal of Accounting and Public Policy* 6 (1987), pp. 75–85.

Levine, R., and D. Renelt. "A Sensitivity Analysis of Cross-Country Growth Regressions." *The American Economic Review* (September 1992), pp. 942–963.

Lucas, R. "On the Mechanics of Economic Development." *Journal of Monetary Economics* (July 1988), pp. 3–42.

Maddison, A. "Growth and Slowdown in Advanced Capitalist Economies: Techniques of Quantitative Assessment." *Journal of Economic Literature* (June 1987), pp. 360–385.

Mankiw, N. G., D. Romer, and D. N. Weil. "A Contribution to the Empirics of Economic Growth." *Quarterly Journal of Economics* (May 1992), pp. 407–437.

Meek, G. K., and S. M. Saudaragaran. "A Survey of Research on Financial Reporting in a Transnational Context." *Journal of Accounting Literature* 9 (1990), pp. 296–314.

Nbudizu, G. A. "Accounting Disclosure Methods and Economic Development: A Criteria for Globalizing Capital Markets." *The International Journal of Accounting* 27 (1992), pp. 151–163.

Plossner, C. I. "The Search for Growth." In *Policies for Long-Run Economic Growth.* Federal Reserve Bank of Kansas, 1992, pp. 57–86.

Prakash, P., and A. Rappaport. "Informational Interdependencies." *The Accounting Review* (October 1975), pp. 723–734.

Ramsey, T. "Test for Specification Errors in Classical Linear Least

Squares Regression Analysis." *Journal of the Royal Statistical Society* 31, Series B (1969), p. 31.

Rebelo, S. "Long-Run Policy Analysis and Long-Run Growth." *Journal of Political Economy* 99 (1991), pp. 500–521.

Riahi-Belkaoui, A. *Accounting Theory*. 3rd ed. London: Academic Press, 1992.

———. *International and Multinational Accounting*. Forth Worth, TX: Dryden Press, 1994.

Romer, P. M. "Increasing Returns and Long-Run Growth." *Journal of Political Economy* (October 1986), pp. 1002–1037.

———. "Capital, Labor, Productivity." In *Brooking Papers on Economic Activity* 2 (1990), pp. 337–420.

———. "Endogenous Technological Change." *Journal of Political Economy* (October 1990), pp. 71–102.

Scott, G. M. "Private Enterprise Accounting in Developing Nations." *International Journal of Accounting* 4 (1968), pp. 51–65.

Solow, R. "A Contribution to the Theory of Economic Growth." *Quarterly Journal of Economics* 70 (1956), pp. 65–94.

Stern, N. "The Determinants of Growth." *The Economic Journal* (January 1991), pp. 122–123.

Stockman, A. "Anticipated Inflation and the Capital Stock in a Cash-in-Advance Economy." *Journal of Monetary Economics* 8 (1981), pp. 387–393.

Talaga, J. A., and G. Ndubizu. "Accounting and Economic Development: Relationship among Paradigms." *International Journal of Accounting Education and Research* 21, 2 (1986), pp. 55–68.

Thursby, J. "A Test for Strategy for Discriminating between Auto-Correlation and Misspecification in Regression Analysis." *Review of Economics and Statistics* 63 (1981), pp. 117–123.

———. "The Relationship among the Specification Test of Hausman, Ramsey and Chow." *Journal of the American Statistical Association* 80 (1985), pp. 926–928.

United Nations. *Human Development Report*. New York: United Nations, 1990.

Wallace, R. S. O., and H. Gernon. "Frameworks for International Comparative Financial Reporting." *Journal of Accounting Literature* 19 (1991), pp. 209–264.

Watts, R. "Corporate Financial Statements, A Product of the Market and Political Processes.'' *Australian Journal of Management* 2 (1977), pp. 53–78.

Watts, R., and J. Zimmerman. ''Towards a Positive Theory of the Determination of Accounting Standards.'' *The Accounting Review* 53 (1978), pp. 112–134.

Wu, P. ''Alternative Tests of Independence between Stochastic Regressors and Disturbances.'' *Econometrics* 2 (1973), pp. 733–750.

3

Political Risk:
Definition and Forecasting

INTRODUCTION

Political risk is a phenomenon that characterizes an unfriendly human climate in both developed and developing countries. A high crime rate or an upsurge of violent unrest, even in highly developed countries, qualifies such countries for the dubious title of "political risk." Political risk essentially refers to the potential economic losses arising as a result of governmental measures or special situations that may either limit or prohibit the multinational activities of a firm. Examples of these situations include those "(1) when discontinuities occur in the business environment, (2) when they are difficult to anticipate, and (3) when they result from political change."[1]

Political risk can affect all foreign firms; in such a case, it is *macropolitical risk*. It may, however, affect only selected foreign firms or industries, or foreign firms with specific characteristics. In such a case it is *micropolitical risk*. In both cases the risk refers to

that uncertainty stemming from unanticipated and unexpected acts of governments or other organizations which may cause a loss to the business firm. It is manifest through a climate of uncertainty dominated by a probable loss to the business enterprise. It may arise from different sources. A wide spectrum of political risks may be generated by the attitudes, policies and overt behavior of those governments and other local power centers such as rival political parties, labor unions, and nationalistic groups.[2]

Political risk may lead to various outcomes, namely expropriation/nationalization, compulsory local equity participation, operational restrictions, discrimination, price controls, blockage of remittances, and breach of government contracts. Given the negative impacts of the outcomes of political risk on foreign operations, especially in the extreme case in which a government takes over a business activity through confiscation and expropriation, there is a strong need to be able to define and forecast political risk. Accordingly, this chapter elaborates on the various attempts in the literature to provide operational definitions of political risk and develop models to forecast political risk.

OPERATIONAL DEFINITIONS OF POLITICAL RISK

Operational definitions of political risk abound. There is no clear consensus on a single definition. The chances or probability of loss; of future occurrence of events or acts; of actions adverse to foreign investments; of potentially significant managerial contingencies; of changes in the operating conditions; and of events, changes, and conditions that will impact on business operations and goals are some of the characteristics of the risk associated with political risk in the literature.[3] One school of thought maintains a differentiation between political and economic risk even though the distinction is not really clear cut. Political risk is viewed as a nonbusiness risk introduced strictly by political forces.[4] Another school of thought prefers to see political risk as part of an overall country risk.[5] Fitzpatrick[6] maintains that the general body of the literature tends to divide into four categories with respect to the definition of political risk as follows:

1. The first category defines political risk in terms of government interference and the unwanted consequences of such action.[7]

2. The second category defines political risk in terms of occurrences of a political nature such as political events or constraints imposed at a specific industry or firm level. Examples of constraints include expropriation, restrictions on remittance of profits, discriminatory taxation, and public sector competition. Examples of political events include government changes and violence.[8]

3. The third category defines political risk in terms of an environment rather than isolation by focusing on changes in either the business environment or political environment.[9]

4. The fourth category considers political risk in a general environment context without a detailed search for or definition of a concept of political risk.

These four categories point to the lack of an operational definition that would be suitable for inclusion in decision making. Kobrin advanced four factors that have limited this operationalization.[10] They are summarized by Fitzpatrick as follows:

First, the distinction between events in the political environment that are of concern to the international business firm and those that are not is ambiguous. Second, it has proved difficult to establish an explicit relationship between environmental processes (continuous versus discontinuous change) and decision makers' perceptions (uncertainty versus risk) to the extent that it can be incorporated into the investment decision model. Third, research literature has concentrated on discontinuous change, with the remaining elements of the political environment receiving only superficial treatment. Fourth, the emphasis in the literature on the negative aspects of government intervention implies an assumption of universal validity, which is doubtful.[11]

TYPOLOGY OF POLITICAL RISK EVENTS

The best way of defining political risk is to associate it with a political risk event. A political risk event is defined by Bunn and Mustafaoglu as any "outcome in the host which, if it occurs, would have a negative impact on the success of the venture."[12] Examples of political risk events are shown in Exhibit 3.1. These political risk events have been classified in the literature as the basis of:

1. The degree of selectivity or discrimination of political risk events as they impact industries, organizations, or projects;[13]
2. The types of groups (actors) which generate them;[14] and
3. The structural and functional elements of an organization.[15]

These three schemes for the classification of political events are shown in Exhibit 3.2.

It is obvious that the most dramatic political risk event is the event of expropriation. Both Kobrin[16] and Minor[17] present evidence of the demise of expropriation by developing countries. Future expropriation activity depends on at least these factors:

• The availability of foreign-owned firms that might be expropriated,
• The feasibility of expropriating, and
• The benefits to the government of expropriation versus alternative policies.[18]

Each of the political events identified is influenced by a host of political risk factors. Examples of political risk factors proposed by Bunn and Mustafaoglu include

1. Sudden ideological change,
2. Visibility of foreigners in economy,
3. Colonial identification of firm,
4. Demonstration effect,
5. Marketing ability,
6. Bureaucratic development,
7. Availability of managerial and scientific technology,
8. Relations with a firm's parent country,

Exhibit 3.1
Examples of Political Risk Events

Change of contract price

Civil disorder (e.g., demonstration, riots, sabotage, terrorism, armed
    insurrection, revolution, guerrilla war, civil war)

Creeping expropriation

Devaluation/revaluation

Domestic price control

Domestic refining and shipping requirements

Embargoes and boycotts

Flow of funds restriction (e.g., dividends, royalties, interest payments, profits,
    repatriation)

Foreign exchange control (e.g., convertability)

Foreign war

Government-to-government sales policies

Hiring and firing constraints (e.g., local employment)

Ideological change

International trade barriers and constraints

Labor relations

Labor shortages

Local product content rules

Locally-shared ownership

Non-tariff barriers (e.g., regulations, subsidies)

Outright nationalization (e.g., confiscation, expropriation)

Production quotas

Reinvestment requirements

Tariff barriers

Tax (e.g., income tax)

Source: Roberto Friedmann and Jonghoon Kim, ''Political Risk and Interna-
    tional Marketing,'' *Columbia Journal of World Business* (Winter 1988),
    p. 65. Copyright 1988. Reprinted with permission.

Exhibit 3.2
Classification Schemes for Political Risk Events

Criteria	Author (Year)	Types of Political Risk Events Identified
1. Selectivity	Robock (1971)	*Macro-political risk* is the one that affects all foreign enterprise, while *micro-political risk* is the one that affects only selected fields of business activity or foreign enterprises with specific characteristics.
	Channon and Jalland (1979)	*Standard regulation intervention* is the one which applies in general to all forms of corporations.
		Discriminatory intervention is the one which discriminates against one corporation in favor of another.
		Selective intervention is applicable to a specific firm, project, or activity.
2. Types of actors	Robock (1971)	Political risk events are generated through groups such as (1) government in power and its operating agencies, (2) parliamentary opposition groups, (3) nonparliamentary opposition groups, (4) nonorganized common interest groups, and (5) foreign governments or intergovernmental agencies.
	Channon and Jalland (1979)	Political risk events are classified by the types of intervening bodies such as (1) the host government, (2) the home government, and (3) a supranational authority.
3. Structural and functional elements of organization	Root (1972)	*Transfer risks* represent host government restrictions on the transfer of capital, payments, products, technology, and persons into or out of the host country.
		Operational risks refer to the interventions that directly constrain the management and performance of local operations in production, marketing, finance, and other business functions.
		Ownership-control risks address the interventions that directly constrain the management and performance of local operations of our international company.

Overholt (1982)   *Asset risks* are those threatening protection of assets.
Organization risks are those threatening control of basic business decisions regarding production, marketing, and personnel management.
Operations risks are those related to access to equipment and raw materials, right to export, and right to import and export funds.
Market risks could threaten the growth of domestic markets, access to foreign markets, and fair competition.

Lax (1983)   *Transfer risks* are the possible government restrictions with respect to the transfer abroad (and sometimes into the host country as well) of capital, profits, technology, personnel, equipment, or the actual commodity produced.
Operational risks represent the possible transit of managerial control to the host government or its chosen representative.
Administrative/statutory risks refer to the likelihood that changes in the regulatory climate will affect a project or agreement.
Ownership risks address questions or equity shares involving issues of participation, expropriation, and nationalization.
Contractual risks cover the bundle of supplies/price issues embodied in nonequity, nonservice-agreement transactions.

Source: Roberto Friedmann and Jonghoon Kim, ''Political Risk and International Marketing,'' *Columbia Journal of World Business* (Winter 1988), pp. 66–67. Copyright 1988. Reprinted with permission.

9. Reciprocal dependence, and

10. Performance of the economy.[19]

A full description of potential risk factors and their associated scenarios is presented in Exhibit 3.3.

EXPLAINING POLITICAL RISK

There are various conceptual approaches to political risk each offering a different lens to view political risk. Friedman and Kim[20] identified six approaches: (a) the actor/source approach, (b) the relative deprivation approach, (c) the product/venture approach, (d) the structural approach, (e) the bargaining power approach, and (f) the government-type approach. They are defined as follows:

1. The actor/source approach explains political risk in terms of different groups and actors causing the political risk.

2. The relative deprivation approach explains political risk in terms of national frustration leading to expropriation.

3. The product/venture approach explains political risk in terms of the different degrees of sensitivity or vulnerability presented by different product or industries.

4. The structural approach explains political risk in terms of the vulnerability of an industry and structural characteristics of that industry, organization, or project.

5. The bargaining power approach explains political risk in terms of the sources of bargaining power for the foreign firm.

6. The government-type approach explains political risk in terms of the risk of radical political change resulted from different types of governmental forms.

The six models for explaining risk are summarized in Exhibit 3.4.

Exhibit 3.3
Political Events and Political Risk Factors

1. *CIVIL DISORDER*
Acts of internal strife evidenced by sabotage, riots: guerilla warfare and civil war can force the suspension of production operations in the host country either by damaging the facilities or by instigating government changes leading to other adverse actions against the company.

1.1 *Strength of Economy*: Poor performance of the domestic economy evidenced by economic measures such as price inflation, unemployment and GNP/capita levels can increase the dissatisfaction of masses causing civil disorder. The chance of civil disorder due to economic reasons is stronger if the country had a fast economic development history and is experiencing a marked stagnation.

1.2 *Aspiration Levels*: The continued discrepencies between the expected and realized standard of living of the population can lead to violent reactions against the government and/or the company which might be used as a scapegoat.

1.3 *Continuity of Leadership*: Lack of a system which permits an orderly transfer of political power can result in violent clashes between rival parties initiating a civil war.

1.4 *Socio-Economic Suppression*: Forced or perceived restriction of upward socio-economic mobility can lead the suppressed groups to resort to civil violence to secure their share of socio-economic benefits.

1.5 *Political Suppression*: The restriction of certain groups within the population from directly participating or indirectly influencing the governmental process can cause acts of civil disorder aimed at political reform.

1.6 *National Coherence*: Civil Disorder results as concensus on fundamental national goals and policies cannot be reached due to the divergence of self-interest groups within the society (e.g., ethnic, religious, political, regional, economic groups).

1.7 *Regime Legitimacy*: If the authority of the present regime is founded upon principles (heredity, parlimentary, etc.) which conflict with the basic values of a portion of the population it may result in use of force to overthrow the regime.

1.8 *Government Corruption*: Groups which perceive themselves as the guardians of justice can resort to violence to overthrow a corrupt government.

1.9 *External Support of Resistance or Liberation Movements*: Foreign military and political support of disruptive movements within the host country can initiate and prolong internal strife.

1.10 *Hostility Toward Our Country*: The deterioration and instability of the relations between our country and the host country exposes the American companies to civil violence by the nationals of the host country.

1.11 *Visibility of Foreigners*: The role and presence of foreign companies is perceived to be highly exploitative making them targets of aggression.

2. *WAR*
The host country's involvement in armed conflict with foreign forces leads to suspension of operations either due to destruction of facilities or by instigating government changes leading to other adverse actions against the company.

2.1 *Ideological Shift*: Due to sudden ideological changes in philosophy (expansionism, socialism, nationalism, etc.) which is incompatible with the neighboring states' policies, armed conflict develops between the host country and the nearby countries which perceive the new regime as a source of regional instability.

2.2 *Threat Negation*: The host country engages in war by launching a pre-emptive attack to negate a threat.

2.3 *Arms Race*: The host country gets involved in war with a neighboring country because it either feels militarily superior or wants to stop the power gap between the two countries from closing.

2.4 *Negative Sanctions*: Imposition of negative sanctions (embargos, prevention of passage, etc.) either on the host country or on a neighboring country by the most country creates a war psychology resulting in armed conflict.

Exhibit 3.3 (continued)

3. SUDDEN EXPROPRIATION
The multinational company's investment is expropriated and the control of operations taken over by the host government. There could be no adequate, inadequate or no compensation.

3.1 *Ideological Change*: There is a sudden change in the host country's ideology (to the extreme left or right) which makes the foreign ownership of key industries incompatible with the conceived economic philosophy of economic sovereignty.

3.2 *Visibility of Foreigners in Economy*: Due to the high visibility of foreigners in economy they are used as scapegoats for the country's ills. Or, the control of the foreign firms on the domestic economy is felt to be highly exploitative that expropriation results.

3.3 *Colonial Identification of Firm*: Although the other firms in the industry are not expropriated, selective expropriation of our firm is effected due to its identification with the previous colonial powers.

3.4 *Demonstration Effect*: The host country follows the trend set by the Third World countries or cartels which expropriate foreign firms within their borders.

3.5 *Marketing Ability*: Either because of strong demand or purposefully developed marketing contacts and skills, the host country expropriates the foreign firms since their market monopoly can be broken.

3.6 *Bureaucratic Development*: The bureaucrats in the host government have the necessary numbers, sophistication and skills to take advantage of economic opportunities by expropriating foreign firms.

3.7 *Availability of Managerial and Scientific Technology*: Either the local technical and managerial talents are well developed or foreign service companies are accessible to enable the government to expropriate and operate the facilities.

3.8 *Relations With Firm's Parent Country*: The deterioration of foreign relationships between the host country and the firm's parent country culminates in the expropriation of firms with the same parent country ownership.

3.9 *Reciprocal Dependence*: There is no or little economic or political interdependence between the host country and the firm's parent country to prevent the expropriation of the multinational.

3.10 *Performance of Economy*: The host country economy performs either very strongly or weakly providing the incentive for the host government to expropriate the foreign firms.

4. CREEPING EXPROPRIATION
The local participation (private and/or public) in the ownership and operation of the company is *gradually* increased to 100% depriving the multinational from the opportunity to realize any returns.

The same factors which contribute to Sudden Expropriation contribute to Creeping Expropriation. The only difference between the factors underlying these two adverse actions is that in the former case the shifts in the factors and their effects are sudden, whereas in the latter case the shifts and effects are gradual.

5. DOMESTIC PRICE CONTROLS
The profitability of the foreign venture is endangered because the host government sets the price of our domestically sold products below the world prices.

5.1 *Domestic Inflation*: Because of spiraling prices, shrinking purchasing power of its citizens and mounting internal pressures, the host government orders mandatory price freezes and/or roll-backs on certain goods including our products.

5.2 *Political Support*: In order to gain domestic political popularity and support, the government imposes controls on our products sold within the country.

84

Exhibit 3.3 (continued)

6. *ADVERSE TAX CHANGES*
   The tax rates on realized revenues are increased by such a magnitude that the original project economics would have dictated the rejection of the venture if the new tax rate were used.

6.1 *Ideological Shift*: A relatively quick change in the political philosophy of host government (either because of a coup or internal pressures) results in higher taxes for the multinational. The planned uses of the additional tax revenues could be comprehensive social welfare, income redistribution and economic development programs.

6.2 *Non-Industry Tax Revenues*: The projected tax revenues from industries other than the one to which our firm belongs are not adequate to finance the ambitious development plans of the host country. Our industry is perceived as not paying enough taxes; and consequently the taxation of firms in this industry is increased.

6.3 *Defense Expenditures*: Tax increases are enacted to finance military expenditures necessitated by armed conflict, arms race or perceived threat from another country.

6.4 *Demonstration Effect*: Following the lead of other Third World countries or cartels, the host country raises the tax rates for our industry.

7. *PRODUCTION RESTRICTIONS*
   Production at efficient rates is restricted due to government regulation. As a result a timely investment recovery and the satisfaction of the minimum corporate return is endangered.

7.1 *Large Income Effects*: The host government reduces the production volumes in order to limit the effects of excessive revenues being pumped into the economy (inflation, import surge, development rate).

7.2 *Investment Absorption Capacity*: The production is restricted by the host government because the available domestic investment opportunities are not numerous enough to absorb the government revenues due to constraints on manpower, in-prefers to defer the revenue buildup for the future by limiting production.

7.3 *Conservation*: The production is restricted for conservation purposes because our product is the only substantial income producing depletable resource of the host country.

7.4 *Production Regulation*: Due to a surplus of our product in the world markets, the host government participates in a production regulation plan with other countries producing the same product to support prices.

8. *PRODUCT EXPORT RESTRICTIONS*
   The export of our products is prohibited or limited for political and economic reasons.

8.1 *Internal Consumption*: The domestic demand for the firm's products forces the government to restrict exports to prevent demand pushed price rises and exchange losses due to additional imports.

8.2 *Participation in an Embargo*: Exports of firm's products to certain countries are prohibited because of the host country's participation in an embargo due to political reasons.

9. *REPATRIATION LIMITATIONS*
   By restricting or excessively delaying the repatriation of profits the host government deprives the multinational the opportunity of investing those funds into higher return projects elsewhere.

9.1 *Balance of Payments*: Continuing deficits in the current account and lack of capital inflows result in restriction of foreign exchange transfers out of the host country.

9.2 *Economic Development*: In order to encourage economic development, the host country forces the foreign firms to reinvest their profits domestically by restricting or prohibiting the transfer of these funds out of the country.

10. *DEVALUATION RISK*
    The devaluation of the host country currency causes exchange losses on the profits to be repatriated.

10.1 *Balance of Payments*: Continued balance of payments deficit forces the government to reduce imports by devaluating the local currency.

10.2 *Decline in Reserve Position*: The decline in monetary reserves (gold, foreign exchange) makes it difficult to convert the local currency into foreign currencies. The government responds by devaluating the local currency.

Exhibit 3.3 (continued)

10.3 *Internal Inflation*: The inflation rate of the host country is greater than that of its major trading partners, causing domestically produced goods to become more expensive than imported items. The government corrects the situation by devaluation.

10.4 *Government Policies Which Treat Symptoms Rather Than Causes*: In the short run, in response to diminishing foreign exchange reserves, government tends to treat symptoms rather than correct fundamental underlying causes. Eventually, devaluation occurs.

10.5 *Economic-Political Policies*: The host government overextends the domestic or international resources of the country (costly wars, welfare programs, labor union militancy, etc.) thus being forced into eventual devaluation.

10.6 *Economic Ties*: The host country's economy is closely tied to another country which devalues its currency forcing the host country to do likewise.

Source: D. W. Bunn and M. M. Mustafaoglu, "Forecasting Political Risk," *Management Science* 24 (November 1978), pp. 1563–1566. Reprinted with permission.

POLITICAL ASSESSMENT MODELS

General Assessment Approaches

When it comes to the forecasting and/or assessment of political risk, a distinction needs to be made between macropolitical risk and micropolitical risk. The distinction is well explicated by Exhibit 3.5. Types A and C refer to macropolitical risk, while Types B and D refer to micropolitical risk. General assessment models covered both macropolitical and micropolitical risks. They are examined next.

Robock and Simmonds suggested an evaluation of the vulnerability of a company to political risk by an analysis of its operations, with the following questions in mind:

- Are periodic external inputs of new technology required?

- Will the project be competing strongly with local nationals who are in, or trying to enter, the same field?

- Is the operation dependent on natural resources, particularly minerals or oil?

- Does the investment put pressure on the country's balance of payments?
- Does the enterprise have a strong monopoly position in the local market?
- Is the product socially essential and acceptable?[21]

Robert Stobaugh noticed that a number of U.S.-based multinational enterprises had developed scales with which to rate countries on the basis of their investment climates.[22] An *Argus Capital Market Report* offered for country risk analysis a laundry list of economic indicators to "educate the decision-maker and force him to think in terms of the relevant economic fundamental."[23] These indicators are monetary base, domestic base, foreign reserves, purchasing power parity index, currency/deposit ratio, consumer prices as a percentage change, balance of payments, goods and services as a percentage of foreign reserves, percentage change exports/percentage change imports, exports as a percentage of the GNP, imports as a percentage of the GNP, foreign factor income payments as a percentage of the GNP, average tax rate, government deficit as a percentage of the GNP, government expenditures, real GNP as a percentage change, and real per capita GNP as a percentage change.

Shapiro offered the following common characteristics of country risk:

1. A large government deficit relative to GDP;
2. A high rate of money expansion if it is combined with a relatively fixed exchange rate;
3. High leverage combined with highly variable terms of trade;
4. Substantial government expenditures yielding low rates of return;
5. Price controls, interest rate ceilings, trade restriction, and other government-imposed barriers to the smooth adjustment of the economy to changing relative price; and
6. A citizenry that demands, and a political system that accepts, government responsibility for maintaining and expanding the nation's

Exhibit 3.4
Conceptual Frameworks for the Explanation of Political Risk

Approaches	Author (Year)	Focus
1. The actor/ source approach	Robock (1971)	The sources of political risk events are (1) competing political philosophies (nationalism, socialism, communism), (2) social unrest or disorder, (3) vested interests of local business groups, (4) recent and impending political independence, (5) armed conflicts and internal rebellions for political power, and (6) new international alliances.
	Boddewyn and Cracco (1972)	Nationalism is the most important underlying factor for political risk (government intervention).
2. The relative deprivation approach	Knudsen (1974a)	A high level of national frustration is the key determinant of expropriation.
	Gurr (1958); Jones (1984)	An empirical investigation of the Venezuelan petroleum industry supports the relative deprivation hypothesis; actions of Venezuelan regimes that reduced the profitability of local U.S. oil production operations were the result of "relative deprivation" experienced by Venezuelans.
3. The product/ venture-type approach	Channon and Jalland (1979); Overholt (1982)	There is a general pattern of the order of different industries according to the degree of political concern.
4. The structural approach	Knudsen (1974b); Truitt (1974); Jodice (1980, 1984); Kobrin (1980)	The vulnerability of an industry, organization, or a project to political risk is mainly dependent on the structural characteristics such as size, localization of management and employment, level of technology to perform various business activities, ownership structure, and host country dependence on the international system.

5. The bargaining power approach	Robock (1971)	The political risk vulnerability of an industry can change due to the degree of the dominance of foreign companies in the sector and the ability of nationals to operate the activities in the industry successfully.
	Fargo and Wells (1982)	The sources of bargaining power for the foreign company are its technology, product differentiation, market access ability, financial resources, product diversity, and the degree of competition.
	Poynter (1984)	The bargaining power sources for the foreign firm are technology, management skills, and exports while those for the host country are its capability to replace the multinational company and its ultimate control over the company.
	Jain (1987)	The bargaining power for the MNCs stems from technology, economies of scale, and product differentiation.
6. The government-type approach	Green (1974)	The risk of radical political change (i.e., the risk of high political instability) is dependent upon the governmental form of the nation.
	Brewer (1981, 1983)	Political instability or risk is associated with a typology of political models: (1) the traditional (state-centric) model of international politics, (2) the pluralistic model of national politics, and (3) the bureaucratic model of intragovernmental politics.

Source: Roberto Friedmann and Jonghoon Kim, ''Political Risk and International Marketing,'' *Columbia Journal of World Business* (Winter 1988), pp. 68–69. Copyright 1988. Reprinted with permission.

Exhibit 3.5
The Nature of Political Risks

Loss contingencies: An involuntary loss of control over specific assets without adequate compensation.	**Type A:** Massive expropriations	**Type B:** Selective nationalizations
Value contingencies: Reduction in the expected value of the benefits to be derived from the foreign affiliate.	**Type C:** General deterioration of the investment climate	**Type D:** Restrictions targeted to key sectors
	Macro risks: Sudden convulsive changes that threaten most of the population of foreign direct investors within the country.	**Micro risks:** Interventions generally motivated by specific consideration closely related to the economic and social conditions prevailing at the time, and to specific industry and firm characteristics.

Source: Reprinted from José de la Torre and David H. Neckar, "Forecasting Political Risks for International Operations," *International Journal of Forecasting* 4 (1988), p. 223, with kind permission from Elsevier Science—NL, Sara Burgerhartstraat 25, 1055 KV Amsterdam, The Netherlands.

standard of living through public sector spending. The less stable the political system, the more important this factor is likely to be.[24]

Rummel and Heenan provided a four-way classification of attempts to forecast political interference: "grand tours," "old hands," Delphi techniques, and quantitative methods.[25] A "grand tour" involves a visit of the potential host country by an executive or a team of people for an inspection tour and later to the home office. Superficiality and overdose of selective information have marred the grand tour technique.

The "old hands" technique involves acquiring area expertise from seasoned educators, diplomats, journalists, or businesspeople. Evidently, too much implicit faith is put in the judgment of these so-called experts.

The Delphi techniques can be used to survey a knowledge group. First, selective elements influencing the political climate are chosen. Next, experts are asked to rank these factors toward the development of an overall measure or index of political risk. Finally, countries are ranked on the basis of the index. As stated by Rummel and Heenan, the "strength of the Delphi technique rests on the posing of relevant questions. When they are defective, the entire structure crumbles."[26]

The quantitative methods technique involves developing elaborate models using multivariate analysis to either explain and describe underlying relationships affecting a nation-sate, or to predict future political events. Two such political risk models using this technique can be identified in the literature and are examined next.

The Knudsen "Ecological" Approach

Harald Knudsen's model involves gathering socioeconomic data depicting the "ecological structures" or investment climate of a particular foreign environment to be used to predict political behavior in general and the national propensity to expropriate in particular[27] (the model is shown in Exhibit 3.6). The model maintains that national propensity to expropriate can be explained by "a national frustration" factor and a "scapegoat function of foreign investment." Basically, if the level of national frustration is high and at the same time the level of foreign investment presence is also high, these foreign investments become a scapegoat, leading to a high propensity to expropriate. The level of frustration is envisaged as the difference between the level of aspirations and the level of welfare and expectations. The scapegoat of foreign investment is determined by the perceived general and special role of foreign investment.

Exhibit 3.6
The National Propensity to Expropriate Model

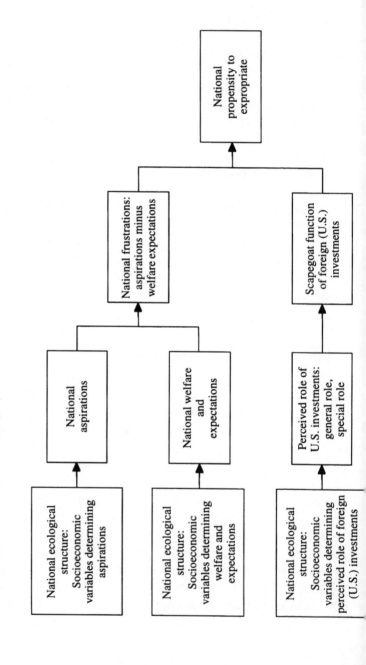

The variables are measured as follows. First, national aspirations can be measured by six proxy variables, namely, degree of urbanization, literacy rate, number of newspapers, number of radios, degree of labor unionization, and the national endowment of national resources. Second, the welfare of people can be measured by proxy variables, namely infant survival rate, caloric consumption, number of doctors per population size, number of hospital beds per population size, percentage of housing with piped water supply, and per capita gross national product. Third, national expectations can be measured by the percentage change in per capita gross national product and the percentage of gross national product being invested. These are surrogate measures of the underlying factors in Knudsen's model. The model's reliability may be improved by a search for more relevant measures by subjecting a larger selection of these surrogate measures to factor analysis. Such as analysis used in a confirmatory way may reduce their number to only the salient measure. But more research, especially in the management accounting field, may be needed to improve and test Knudsen's model or similar "components-based" models of predicting political risk.

The Haendel-West-Meadow "Political System Stability Index"

Another components approach to the forecasting of political risk was provided by Haendel, West, and Meadow in an empirical, indicator-based measure of political system stability, the political system stability index (PSSI), in 65 developing countries.[28] It is composed of three equally weighted indices: the socioeconomic index, the governmental process index, and the societal conflict index, which is itself derived from three sub-subindices on public unrest, internal violence, and coercion potential. All of these indices are derived from 15 indirect measures of the political system: stability and adaptability. Basically, the higher the PSSI score, the greater the stability of the political system. The index was based on data from the 1961–66 period.

There is a need to test the validity of the index with more recent data before using it as a forecasting tool. In any case, the model demonstrates again the feasibility of a components approach to the study of political risk. As stated by Haendel, the political system stability index derives its importance from the role the political system plays in establishing power relationships and norms for resolving conflicts in society. It assumes that the degree of political stability in a country may indicate the society's capacity to cope with new demands.[29]

Classification of Political Risk Models

Various classifications of political risk models exist in the literature. They are examined next.

A. The first classification of political assessment methodologies is a review by Kobrin,[30] and a comparison in terms of their degree of structure (explicit model of process) and systematization (formalization of methodology). A major distinction is made between *observational* and *expert-generated* data. The latter are then classified in terms of *structure* and *systematization*. Observational data in formal models refer to reliance on data from secondary sources. These economic and/or potential data, derived from secondary sources, are used to develop formal models of political macrorisks, especially by service organizations.

Methodologies based on expert-generated data can be classified as the basis of their degree of structure and systematization:

a. The structure refers to the presence of an explicit conceptual model of the process linking political events and managerial contingencies. The methodology may be either structured or unstructured. They are defined as follows:

An unstructured methodology is *subjective* in that assumptions are not made explicit and the modeling of relationships is intuitive in the sense that it takes place at an unconscious level. A structured methodology is *objective* in the sense that assumptions and the model of process relating cause and effect are explicit.[31]

b. The systematization refers to the degree of formalization of the forecasting methodology. The systematization can be either explicit or implicit. They are defined as follows:

A systematic methodology involves explicit, although not necessarily elegant or sophisticated, assessment and/or forecasting procedures. An intuitive or implicit forecasting methodology relies on the mental process of the forecaster and is difficult to replicate.[32]

The expert-based methodologies include, therefore, three political options:
 1. Unstructured/unsystematic assessments that rely on implicit conceptual and analytical methodologies. Kobrin gives the example of a U.S. firm establishing a political assessment unit staffed by ex-foreign service officers, which produced a political report on Brazil.[33]
 2. Unstructured/systematic assessments that rely on some degree of formalization and a checklist to guide the evaluation of country risk. Kobrin gives the example of two analytical approaches that entail a greater degree of formalization, but still lack structure.[34] They are the BERI index provided by BERI service and the ESP (economic, social, and political) system of a large chemical company.
 3. Structured/systematic assessments that rely on objective and explicit analytical methodologies. Kobrin gives the example of the World Political Risk Forecast (WPRF) offered by Frost and Sullivan and the number of approaches evolving from the ASPRO/SPAIR system developed by Shell Oil.[35]
 B. The second classification of political assessment methodologies is provided by de la Torre and Neckaar,[36] as the basis of the models' orientation and their geographic scope. As shown in Exhibit 3.7, the models can be classified as two dimensions: one dimension covering the continuum from few to many countries, and one dimension covering the continuum from general (macro) orientation to specific (micro) orientation. It is important to notice the absence of models examining micropolitical risk for

Exhibit 3.7
Political Forecasting Models Classified by Their Orientation and Their Geographic Scope

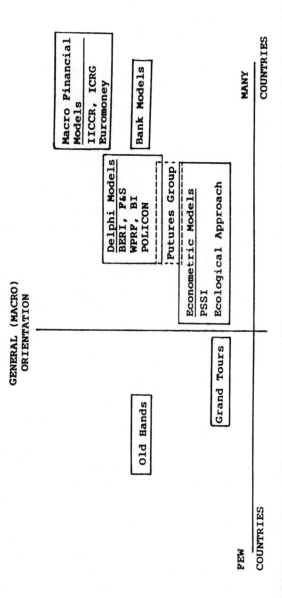

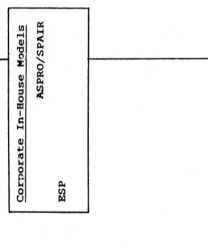

Corporate In-House Models

ESP

ASPRO/SPAIR

SPECIFIC (MICRO)
ORIENTATION

Source: Reprinted from José de la Torre and David H. Neckar, "Forecasting Political Risks for International Operations," *International Journal of Forecasting* 4 (1988), p. 230, with kind permission from Elsevier Science—NL, Sara Burgerhartstraat 25, 1055 KV Amsterdam, The Netherlands.

many countries, as evidenced by the absence of models in the bottom right-hand corner of the exhibit. The models classified include the usual expert-based systems, in-house methods, and econometric methods. All of them have certain strengths and limitations. As stated by de la Torre and Neckar:

Expert-based systems can be criticized for not always making causal relationships explicit and for their potential bias in the judgement of its members. Econometric models often suffer from the difficulty of securing current sources of data for many of the important independent variables necessary for the analysis. In-house methods can be expensive, time consuming and of little geographic coverage.[37]

Composition of Existing Political Risk Models

Political risk assessment is a must in any strategic planning process of multinational corporations. It usually exists in the form of a letter grade or numerical score for a country as a whole that can be used by investors and managers in other decision making. The numerical scores are produced by various institutions and share the merit of providing a quantitative guide to political risk. In developing the score, the forecaster tried to link the act resulting in a loss to the causes of the act. Examples of loss actions include the following:

- Expropriation or nationalization of property or resources,
- Inconvertibility of currency (profits),
- War damage,
- Civil strife damage,
- Breach of contract for political reasons or by a political body,
- Damage to property,
- Actions against personnel (such as kidnaping),
- Limits on remittances,
- Government interference with terms of a contract,
- Discriminatory taxation,

- Politically based regulations on operations, and
- Loss of copyright protection.[38]

What constitutes a model of political risk is the exact determination of what variables or circumstances can explain or predict these losses. To illustrate the process of construction of such indices, three models of political risk assessment are described, namely, (a) the assessment by the *Economist*,[39] (b) the business environment risk intelligence (BERI) political risk index (PRI), and (c) the political risk services (PRS) system.[40]

A. *The Economist Method* rests as a 100-point index of risk, with 33 attributed to economic factors, 50 to politics, and 17 to society.

1. The economic factors include (a) falling GDP per person, (b) high inflation, (c) capital flight, (d) high and rising debt, (e) decline in food production per person, and (f) raw materials as a high percentage of exports.
2. The political variables include (a) bad neighbors (3 negative points), (b) authoritarianism (7 points), (c) stallness (5 points), (d) illegitimacy (9 points), (e) generals in power (6 points), and (f) over/armed insurrection (20 points).
3. The social variables include (a) urbanization pace (3 points), (b) Islamic fundamentalism (4 points), (c) corruption (6 points), and (d) ethnic tension (4 points).

B. *The BERI Political Risk Index (PRI)* rests on scores assigned to 10 political variables by experts on a seven-point scale with potential added bonus points to bring a possible total of 100. The 10 variables are divided into (a) "Internal Causes of Political Risk," (b) "External Causes of Political Risk," and (c) "Symptoms of Political Risk." The internal causes include the following variables:

1. Factionalization of the political spectrum and the power of these factions;

2. Factionalization by language, ethnic, and/or religious groups and the power of these factions;

3. Restrictive (coercive) measures required to retain power;

4. Mentality, including xenophobia, nationalism, corruption, nepotism, and willingness to compromise;

5. Social conditions, including extremes in population density and the distribution of wealth; and

6. Organization and strength of forces for a radical left government.

The external causes include the following:

1. Dependence on and/or importance to a hostile major power, and

2. Negative influences of regional political forces.

The symptoms of political risk include the following:

1. Societal conflict involving demonstrations, strikes, and street violence, and

2. Instability as perceived by nonconstitutional changes, assassinations, and guerilla wars.

The BERI index is to be interpreted as follows:

1. 70–100 indicates a stable environment of a low-risk advanced industrialized economy,

2. 55–69 indicates a moderate-risk country with complications in day-to-day operations,

3. 40–54 indicates a high-risk country for foreign-arrived businesses, and

4. 0–39 indicates unacceptable conditions for foreign-owned businesses.

C. *The Political Risk Services (PRS)* index rests on experts' predictions and a modified Delphi technique.[41] The variables examined by the experts include the following: (a) political turmoil probability, (b) equity restrictions, (c) personnel/procurement interference, (d) taxation discrimination, (e) repatriation restrictions, (f) exchange controls, (g) tariff imposition, (h) nontariff/barrier imposition, (i) payment delays, (j) fiscal/monetary expansion, (k) labor cost expansion, and (l) international borrowing.

A Framework for Modeling Political Risk

A framework for modeling political risk ought to make a distinction between the analysis of macrorisk and its application for the analysis of microrisk. In other words, the political risk should be modeled for macrorisk to be able to predict potential events that can affect specific projects and lead to potential outcomes. De la Torre and Neckar present such a framework.[42] It is shown in Exhibit 3.8. Basically, a series of national characteristics, comprising economic, social, and political forces at work, can be modeled using econometric models or experts' methods to explain and/or predict political stability and political risk. This phase of the framework constitutes stage 1 of the analysis of macrorisks and the derivation of a political risk model. The events predicted by the model can (a) have an impact on project characteristics including industry factors, corporate factors, structural factors, and managerial factors, and (b) generate potential outcomes of interest to multinational firms. This phase of the framework constitutes stages of the analysis microrisks. The application of both stages of risk analysis is a determination of the total risk profile, which is summarized in Exhibit 3.9. A detailed list of the factors used for country-associated risk is shown in Exhibit 3.10. Another detailed list of factors used in project associated risk is shown in Exhibit 3.11.

CONCLUSIONS

This chapter is a review of the literature on the definition and forecasting of political risk. Various definitions and explanations of political risk abound, which explains the varieties of political

Exhibit 3.8
A Conceptual Model for Project-Specific Risk Analysis

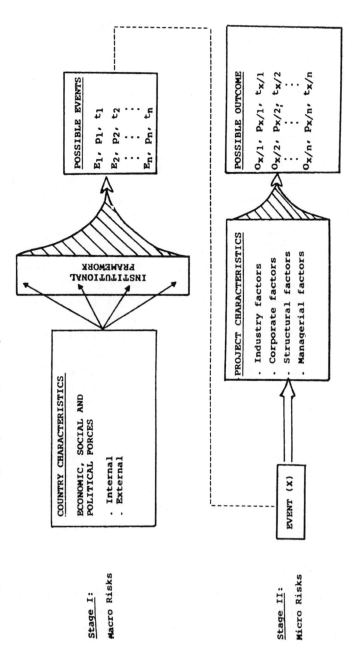

Source: Reprinted from José de la Torre and David H. Neckar, "Forecasting Political Risks for International Operations," *International Journal of Forecasting* 4 (1988), p. 231, with kind permission from Elsevier Science—NL, Sara Burgerhartstraat 25, 1055 KV Amsterdam, The Netherlands.

Major Variables (Factors) for Assessing Project-Specific Political Risk

Source: Reprinted from José de la Torre and David H. Neckar, "Forecasting Political Risks for International Operations," *International Journal of Forecasting* 4 (1988), p. 233, with kind permission from Elsevier Science—NL, Sara Burgerhartstraat 25, 1055 KV Amsterdam, The Netherlands.

Exhibit 3.10
Content of Country Risk Variables

	COUNTRY ASSOCIATED RISK	
	ECONOMIC FACTORS	**POLITICAL FACTORS**

INTERNAL	Population and income
	-size and sectoral distribution
	-economic growth and per capita income
	-population growth and control
	-income distribution
	
	Workforce and employment
	-size and composition
	-sectoral and geographic distribution
	-productivity
	-migration and urban unemployment
	
	Sectoral analysis
	-agriculture and self-sufficiency
	-industrial growth and distribution
	-size and growth of the public sector
	-national priorities and strategic sectors
	
	Economic geography
	-natural resources
	-economic diversification
	-topography and infrastructure
	
	Government and social services
	-sources and structure of government
	  revenues
	-sectoral and geographic pattern of
	  expenditures
	-size and growth of the budget deficit
	-rigidities in spending programs
	-regional dependency on central
	  revenue sources
	
	General indicators
	-price indices
	-wage rates
	-interest rates, money supply, etc.
		Composition of population
		-ethnolinguistic, religious, tribal or class
		  heterogenity
		-relative shares in economic and political
		  power
		-immigration and outmigration
		
		Culture
		-underlying cultural values and beliefs
		-religious and moral values
		-sense of alienation with foreign or
		  modern influences
		
		Government and institutions
		-constitutional principles and conflicts
		-resilience of national institutions
		-role and strength of the army, church,
		  parties, press, educational establishment, etc
		
		Power
		-key leaders' background and attitudes
		-main beneficiaries of the status quo
		-role and power of the internal security
		  apparatus
		
		Opposition
		-strength, sources of support, effectiveness
		
		General indicators
		-level and frequency of strikes
		-riots and terrorist acts
		-number and treatment of political prisoners
		-extent of official corruption

104

EXTERNAL	**Foreign trade & invisibles**	**Alignments**
	-current account balance and composition -income and price elasticity of exports and imports -price stability of major imports and exports -evolution of the terms of trade -geographic composition of trade	-international treaties and alignments -position on international issues, UN voting record
	External debt and servicing	**Financial support**
	-outstanding foreign debt, absolute and relative levels -terms and maturity profile -debt servicing to income and exports	-financial aid, food and military assistance -preferential economic and trade linkages
	Foreign investment	**Regional ties**
	-size and relative importance -sectoral distribution -geographic (by origin) and regional distribution	-border disputes -external military threat or guerrilla activities -nearby revolution, political refugees
	Overall balance of payments	**Attitude towards foreign capital and investment**
	-trends in the capital account -reserve position -capital flight and "errors and omissions"	-national investment codes -polls of local attitudes towards foreign investors -court proceedings in disputes
	General indicators	**General indicators**
	-exchange rates (official and unofficial) -changes in international borrowing terms	-record on human rights -formal exiled opposition groups -terrorist acts in third countries -diplomatic or commercial conflict with home country

Source: Reprinted from José de la Torre and David H. Neckar, "Forecasting Political Risks for International Operations," *International Journal of Forecasting* 4 (1988), p. 234, with kind permission from Elsevier Science—NL, Sara Burgerhartstraat 25, 1055 KV Amsterdam, The Netherlands.

Exhibit 3.11
Content of Project Risk Variables

PROJECT-ASSOCIATED RISK

INDUSTRY FACTORS	**Activity/economic sector** • higher exposure in primary and infrastructure projects • size of project, relative importance, monopoly power • national priorities (e.g., high technology sectors) **Technology** • R&D intensity and rate of change of technology • alternative suppliers, relative quality **Product differentiation** • specialized inputs, distinctiveness • service industry **Competition** • largest risk when competition is nonexistent or very active
CORPORATE FACTORS	**Nationality** • ex-colonial relationships • home/host country diplomatic and commercial relations **Scope of activities** • sectoral nature of corporate activities • geographic distribution of affiliates **Corporate image** • corrupt payments scandals • previous involvement in political subversion • past record as corporate citizen **Previous losses** • patterns of bargaining and losses • instances of survival

STRUCTURAL
FACTORS

Contribution to the local economy

- positive factors include capital, employment creation, income and tax revenues, reinvestment, substitution effects, export generation, local industrial development, etc.
- negative effects are dividends and capital repatriation, licensing, management and technical fees, transfer pricing, import generation, competitive effects, etc.
- social cost/benefit analysis
- special agreements and investment code exceptions
- timing, the obsolescing bargain

Intracorporate transfers

- degree of integration with parent company network
- local-for-local affiliate

Local ownership

- share and nature of domestic partners

Environmental dissonance

- geographic location
- ethnic, environmental, and linguistic risks
- cultural compatibility

MANAGERIAL
FACTORS

Local management

- extent and positions of local managers

Corporate culture and management philosophy

- experience, training, and sensitivity of expatriates
- headquarters' respect for local opinion, decentralization

Political responsiveness

- degree of activism by local management
- local contacts, lobbying, public affairs

Financial policies

- exposure reduction vs. provocation

Source: Reprinted from José de la Torre and David H. Neckar, "Forecasting Political Risks for International Operations," *International Journal of Forecasting* 4 (1988), p. 235, with kind permission from Elsevier Science—NL, Sara Burgerhartstraat 25, 1055 KV Amsterdam, The Netherlands.

assessment models provided. A modeling of political risk requires a destruction between the modeling of macropolitical risk and the use of the resulting model in predicting and/or explaining the outcomes resulting from micropolitical risk. The modeling of macropolitical risk needs to take into account internal and external economic and sociopolitical factors. The choice of diagnostic internal and external economic and sociopolitical factors is essential to the success and the reliability of the political risk model. Such a model is proposed in the next chapter.

NOTES

1. S. H. Robock and K. Simmonds, *International Business and Multinational Enterprises* (Homewood, IL: Irwin, 1973), p. 356.

2. Fred Greene, "Management of Political Risk," *Best's Review* (July 1974), p. 15.

3. Roberto Friedmann and Jonghoon Kim, "Political Risk and International Marketing," *Columbia Journal of World Business* (Winter 1988), p. 64.

4. D. A. Jodice, "Trends in Political Risk Assessment: Prospects for the Future," in *International Political Risk Management: New Dimensions*, ed. Fariborz Ghadar and Theodore H. Moran (New York: Ghadar and Associates, 1984), pp. 8–26.

5. Charles M. Newman II and I. James Czechowicz, *International Risk Management* (Morristown, NJ: Financial Executive Research Foundation, 1983).

6. Mark Fitzpatrick, "The Definition and Assessment of Political Risk in International Business: A Review of the Literature," *Academy of Management Review* 8 (1983), pp. 249–254.

7. P. Ady, *Private Foreign Investment and the Developing World* (New York: Praeger, 1972).

8. B. M. Bass, D. W McGregor, and J. L. Walters, "Selecting Foreign Plant Sites: Economic, Social, and Political Considerations," *Academy of Management Journal* 4 (1977), pp. 535–551.

9. Stefan H. Robock, "Political Risk: Identification and Assessment," *Columbia Journal of World Business* 6 (1971), pp. 6–20.

10. S. J. Kobrin, "Political Risk: A Review and Reconsideration," *Journal of International Business Studies* 10, 1 (1979), pp. 67–80.

11. Fitzpatrick, "The Definition and Assessment of Political Risk in International Business," p. 251.

12. D. W. Bunn and M. M. Mustafaoglu, "Forecasting Political Risk," *Management Science* (November 1978), p. 1558.

13. D. F. Channon and M. Jalland, *Multinational Strategic Planning* (London: The Macmillan Press Ltd., 1979).

14. S. H. Robock, "Political Risk: Identification and Assessment," pp. 6–20.

15. Howard L. Lax, *Political Risk in the International Oil and Gas Industry* (Boston: International Human Resources Development Corporation, 1983).

16. S. J. Kobrin, "Expropriation as an Attempt to Control Foreign Firms in LDCs: Trends for 1960–1979," *International Studies Quarterly* (September 1984), pp. 329–348.

17. M. S. Minor, "The Demise of Expropriation as an Investment of LCD Policy, 1980–1992," *Journal of International Business Studies* 25, 1 (1994), pp. 177–188.

18. Bunn and Mustafaoglu, "Forecasting Political Risk," p. 1559.

19. Ibid.

20. Friedmann and Kim, "Political Risk and International Marketing," pp. 66–67.

21. Robock and Simmonds, *International Business and Multinational Enterprises*, p. 371.

22. Robert Stoubagh, Jr., "How to Analyze Foreign Investment Climates," *Harvard Business Review* (September–October 1969), pp. 101–102.

23. "A Primer on Country Risk," *Argus Capital Market Report* (June 4, 1975), pp. 15–25.

24. Alan C. Shapiro, "Currency Risk and Country Risk in International Banking," *The Journal of Finance* (July 1985), p. 891.

25. R. J. Rummel and David A. Heenan, "How Multinationals Analyze Political Risk," *Harvard Business Review* (January–February 1978), pp. 67–76.

26. Ibid., p. 70.

27. Harald Knudsen, "Explaining the National Propensity to Expropriate: An Ecological Approach," *Journal of International Business Studies* 4, 7 (Spring 1974), pp. 51–71.

28. Dan Haendel and Gerald T. West with Robert G. Meadow, *Overseas Investment and Political Risk*, Monograph Series, no. 21 (Philadelphia, PA: Foreign Policy Research Institute, 1957).

29. Dan Haendel, *Foreign Investments and the Management of Political Risk* (Boulder, CO: Westview Press, 1979), pp. 106–107.

30. Stephen Korbin, "Political Assessment by International Firms: Models or Methodologies?" *Journal of Policy Modeling* 3 (1981), pp. 251–270.

31. Ibid., p. 256.

32. Ibid.

33. Ibid., p. 259.

34. Ibid., p. 260.

35. Ibid., p. 262.

36. José de la Torre and David H. Neckar, "Forecasting Political Risk for International Operations," *International Journal of Forecasting* 4 (1988), pp. 221–241.

37. Ibid., p. 231.

38. L. D. Howell and B. Chaddick, "Models of Political Risk for Foreign Investment and Trade: An Assessment of Three Approaches," *Columbia Journal of World Business* (Fall 1994), p. 73.

39. "Countries in Trouble," *The Economist* (December 20, 1986), pp. 25–28.

40. W. D. Coplin and M. K. O'Leary, *Introduction to Political Risk Analysis* (Croton-on-Hudson, NY: Policy Studies Associates, 1983).

41. W. D. Coplin, M. K. O'Leary, and T. Sealy, *A Business Guide to Political Risk for International Decisions*, 2nd ed. (Syracuse, NY: Political Risk Services, 1991).

42. de la Torre and Neckar, "Forecasting Political Risks for International Operations," pp. 221–241.

SELECTED READINGS

Baglini, Norman A. *Global Risk Management: How US International Corporations Manage Foreign Risks*. New York: Risk Management Society Publishing, 1983.

Boddewyn, Jean, and Etienne F. Cracco. "The Political Game in World Business." *Columbia Journal of World Business* 7 (January–February 1972), pp. 45–56.

Brewer, Thomas L. "Political Risk Assessment for Foreign Direct Investment Decisions: Better Methods for Better Results." *Columbia Journal of World Business* 16 (Spring 1981), pp. 5–13.

————. "Political Sources of Risk in the International Money Markets: Conceptual, Methodological, and Interpretive Refinements." *Journal of International Business Studies* 14 (Spring–Summer 1983), pp. 161–64.

Bunn, D. W., and M. M. Mustafaoglu. "Forecasting Political Risk." *Management Science* 24 (November 1978), pp. 1557–1567.

Channon, Derek F., and Michael Jalland. *Multinational Strategic Planning*. London: The Macmillan Press Ltd., 1979.

Farge, Nathan, and Louis T. Wells, Jr. "Bargaining Power of Multinational and Host Governments." *Journal of International Business Studies* 13 (Fall 1982), pp. 9–23.

Green, Robert T. "Political Structures as a Predicator of Radical Political Change." *Columbia Journal of World Business* 9 (Spring 1974), pp. 28–36.

Gurr, Ted Robert. "A Causal Model of Civil Strife: A Comparative Analysis Using New Indices." *American Political Science Review* 62 (December 1968), pp. 1104–1124.

Jain, Subhash C. *International Marketing Management*. 2nd ed. Boston: Kent Publishing, 1987.

Jodice, David A. "Sources of Change in Third World Regimes for Foreign Direct Investment, 1968–1976." *International Organization* 34 (Spring 1980), pp. 177–206.

————. "Trends in Political Risk Assessment: Prospects for the Future." In *International Political Risk Management: New Dimensions*, ed. Fariborz Ghadar and Theodore H. Moran. New York: Ghadar and Associates, 1984, pp. 8–26.

Jones, Randall J. "Empirical Models of Political Risks in US Oil Production Operations in Venezuela." *Journal of International Business Studies* 15 (Spring–Summer 1984), pp. 81–95.

Knudsen, Harold J., "Explaining the National Propensity to Expropriate: An Ecological Approach." *Journal of International Business Studies* 4, 7 (Spring 1974), pp. 51–71.

————. *Expropriation of Private Foreign Investment in Latin America*. Bergen, Norway: Universitetsforlaget, 1974.

Kobrin, Stephen J. "When Does Political Instability Result in Increased Investment Risk?" *Columbia Journal of World Business* 13 (Fall 1978), pp. 113–122.

————. "Foreign Enterprise and Forced Divestment in Less Developed Countries." *International Organization* 34 (Winter 1980), pp. 65–88.

————. *Managing Political Risk Management*. Berkeley: University of California Press, 1982.

Lax, Howard L. *Political Risk in the International Oil and Gas Industry*. Boston: International Human Resources Development Corporation, 1983.

Merrill, James. "Country Risk Analysis." *Columbia Journal of World Business* 17 (Spring 1982), pp. 88–91.

Newman, Charles M., II and I. James Czechowicz. *International Risk Management*. Morristown, NJ: Financial Executive Research Foundation, 1983.

O'Leary, Michael K., and William D. Coplin. *Political Risk in Thirty Five Countries*. 1983 ed. London: Euromoney Publications Limited, 1983.

Overholt, William H. *Political Risk*. London: Euromoney Publications, 1982.

Poynter, Thomas A. "Managing Political Risk: A Strategy for Defending the Subsidiary." In *International Political Risk and Management: New Dimensions*, ed. Fariborz Ghadar and Theodore H. Moran. New York: Ghadar and Associates, 1984, pp. 138–150.

Robock, Stefan H. "Political Risk: Identification and Assessment." *Columbia Journal of World Business* 6 (July–August 1971), pp. 6–20.

Root, Franklin R. "Analyzing Political Risks in International Business." In *The Multinational Enterprise in Transition*, ed. A. Kapoor and Philip D. Grub. Princeton, NJ: The Darwin Press, 1972, pp. 354–365.

Shapiro, Alan C. "Managing Political Risk: A Policy Approach." *Columbia Journal of World Business* 16 (Fall 1981), pp. 63–69.

Simon, Jeffrey D. "Political Risk Assessment: Past Trends and Future Prospects." *Columbia Journal of World Business* 17 (Fall 1982), pp. 62–71.

4

The Determinants of Political Risk: A Model

INTRODUCTION

Political risk in general and political risk ratings in particular are of importance to managers of multinational firms eager to take political risk into account in their expansion capital budgeting, mergers, and other decisions. It would be much more practical and useful if these managers were able to not only rely on existing political risk ratings but also to replicate the same rating using an established political risk prediction model. Accordingly, it is the objective of this chapter to offer a political risk prediction model that replicates a known political risk index. The model, as suggested in the first three chapters, relies on economic and political variables that describe those aspects of the political and economic environment most linked to political risk.

POLITICAL RISK VARIABLES

The dependent variable is a political risk index. Various country risk ratings exist that pose choice problems. The measure includes the following:

1. *Euromoney* issues a credit rating score that is a weighted average of three indicators: (a) market indicators that cover ac-

cess to bond markets, sell down performance, and access to trade financing (40 percent); (b) credit indicators that include payment record and rescheduling problems (20 percent); and (c) analytical indicators that cover political risk and economic performance and conditions (40 percent).

2. Institutional investors issue a country credit worthiness score based on ratings provided by leading international banks, who are asked to assign a grade to each country in a scale of 0 (not credit worthy) to 100 (most credit worthy). The individual responses are then weighted according to an unpublished formula to produce a country creditworthiness score.

3. The *International Country Risk Guide* (ICRG) of International Business Communication Ltd. produces risk rating scores that receive the most attention from foreign visitors. ICRG provides a composite risk rating as well as individual ratings for political, financial, and economic risk. The political component, which makes up 50 percent of the composite score, includes factors such as government corruption and how economic expectations diverge from reality. The financial component includes such factors as the likelihood of losses from exchange controls and loan defaults. Finally, the economic component includes such factors as inflation and debt service costs. The maximum, or least risky, score is 100 for the political category and 50 each for the financial and economic risks. For the composite score, 85–100 is considered very low risk; 70–84.5 is low risk; 60–69.5 is moderate risk; 50–59.5 is moderately high risk; and 0–49.5 is very high risk.

This brief description of the three risk measures indicates that the best candidate for a dependent variable is the political risk component of the ICRG. It is used in this study.

EXPLANATORY VARIABLES

The set of explanatory variables is derived from descriptive and empirical studies of the political environment and economic environment, as described in Chapters 1 and 2, and of political risk, as described in Chapter 3. A description of these explanatory variables follows.

Human Development Index

Just as economic growth is necessary for a reduction of political risk, human development is also critical to lessening political risk. Human development is hampered by conditions of poverty, malnutrition, ill health, inadequate education, and gender disparities. When people face low human development conditions, they are less likely to be able to devote the resources and energy to create a politically stable environment. Obstacles to human development are also obstacles to a reduction in political risk. Human development is generally measured by the UN human development index (HDI), which is generally considered a more realistic measure of human development than mere GNP per head. The HDI is composed of three indicators: life expectancy, education, and income. The detailed computation of the index is shown in the Appendix. In the context of the prediction of political risk, the expected sign of the HDI is positive. *The higher the human development conditions, as measured by HDI, the higher the political stability, as measured by the political risk index.*

Gross Domestic Savings as a Percentage of Gross Domestic Product

Economic theory holds that higher rates of savings and investment are crucial to the long rate growth of an economy.[1] Solov's framework[2] implies that a high investment on savings rate results in higher accumulated capital per worker and leads to an increase in the per capita output of the economy.

The linear stage of economic growth focuses on the importance to development of both the acquisition and use of capital and the historical development of the developed countries. One example is Rostow's argument that the advanced countries have passed the stage of "takeoff into self-sustaining growth," while the underdeveloped countries are in a "preconditions" stage and in need of massive infusion of domestic and foreign savings before growth takes place.[3] A second example is the *Harrod-Domar growth model*, which simply states that the growth of national income will be directly, or positively, related to the savings ratio, and inversely, or negatively, related to the economy's capital/output ratio. None of these theories and models work effectively for the developing countries because more savings and investments are not sufficient or economic growth. Favorable institutional and attitudinal conditions need to be present before takeoff can take place. In Chapter 2, we showed that gross domestic investment, as a percentage of gross domestic product, is positively associated with economic growth. This result is consistent with endogenous growth models, with an emphasis on broader concepts of capital, such as those of Rebelo[4] and Barro,[5] who argue that per capita growth and the investment ratio tend to move together. It can be easily argued that gross domestic savings or investment, as a percentage of gross domestic product, is a positive determinant of political stability. *Therefore, the higher the gross domestic savings, as a percentage of gross domestic product, the higher the political stability, measured by the political risk index.*

Labor Force as a Percentage of Total Population

A domestic problem that can affect political risk is that of unemployment. In the developing countries, not only is a very large section of the population unemployed, but unemployment seems to grow faster than employment, mainly due to the phenomenon of labor underutilization. Edgar Edwards distinguishes among the following forms of underutilization of labor: open unemployment; underemployment; the visible active but underutilized as disguised underemployment, hidden unemployment, and prematurely retired; the impaired; and the unproductive.[6] All major economic models of employment determination are advocated in the literature, namely, classical, Keynesian, the output/employment macromodel, the price-incentive micromodel, and the two-sector labor transfer model.

The classical model relies on the forces of supply and demand to set the wage rate and the level of employment. The Keynesian model relies on demand factors such as increases in government expenditures and encouragement of private investments to reduce unemployment. Both the classical and the Keynesian models are considered to be far from relevant to the developing countries. The output/employment macromodel argues that the rate of national output and employment depend on the rate of savings and investment, lending credence to the "big push" for industrialization in some developing countries. The price incentive model maintains that the combination of labor and capital will be dictated by the relative factor prices. Cheap labor would lead to labor intensive production processes. Finally, the two-sector labor transfer of rural urban migration focuses on the determinants of both demand and supply.

Two variations characterize the last model: the Lewis theory of development[7] and the Todaro model.[8] The Lewis model divides the economy in two sectors: (1) as a traditional, rural subsistence sector characterized by zero- or low-productivity surplus labor and (2) as a growing urban industrial sector characterized by an influx of labor from the subsistence sector. The Todaro model hypothesizes that migration is due to urban-rural differences in expected rather than actual earnings. All these approaches lead to a consensus position on employment strategy, which would include the following five elements: (1) creating an appropriate rural-urban economic balance; (2) expanding small-scale, labor-intensive industries; (3) eliminating factor-price distortions; (4) choosing appropriate labor-intensive technologies of production; and (5) noting the direct linkage between education and employment.[9]

The above analysis on the importance of unemployment posits the need to have a high labor price as a percentage of total population as a determinant of economic growth in general and political stability in particular. *Therefore, the higher the labor force, as a percentage of total population, the higher the political stability, measured by the political risk index.*

Terms of Trade

Developing countries suffer from two main limitations in their trading with developed countries. First, their exports are heavily composed of nonnumerical primary products, while their imports include everything from new materials to capital goods, intermediate producer goods, and consumer products. Second, the commodity terms of trade, measured by the ratio between the price of a typical unit of exports and the price of a typical unit of imports, are deteriorating. The result shows up in a continuous deficit in the current and capital accounts of their balance of payments. To solve this problem a variety of options are used: export promotion or import substitution policies; encouragement of private foreign investment, or call for public and private foreign assistance; greater use of the Special Drawing Rights of the International Monetary Fund (IMF); foreign exchange controls or currency devaluation; economic integration with other developing countries in the form of customs unions, free-trade areas, or common markets.[10] But above all, the major option is the choice of a trade strategy for development. Should it be an outward- or inward-looking policy? An outward-looking policy results from the classical trade theory and comparative cost advantage arguments with the implication that free trade will maximize global output by allowing every country to specialize in what it does best. P. P. Streeten states that point as follows: "Outward-looking policies encourage not only free trade but also the free movement of capital, workers, enterprises and students, a welcome to the multinational enterprise, and open system of communications. If it does not imply laissez-faire, it certainly implies *laissez-passer.*"[11]

An inward-looking policy results from the belief that the developing countries should be encouraged to engage in their own style of development and not be constrained by or dependent on foreign importation, and to learn by doing. Streeten explains this option as follows: Inward-looking policies emphasize the need for an indigenous technology, appropriate for the factors available in the country, and for an appropriate range of products. If you keep out the multinational enterprise, with its wrong technology, you will evolve your own style of development and you will be a stronger, more independent master of your own fate.[12]

In short, an outward-looking policy is identifiable with export promotion while an inward-looking policy is identifiable with import substitution. These two strategies, when added to the strategies of primary and secondary or manufacturing production, yield a fourfold division: primary outward-looking policies, secondary outward-looking policies, primary inward-looking policies, and secondary inward-looking policies.[13] The choice of any one of these options determines the nature of international trade of each developing country and of its impact on development.

Export promotion is good for economic growth, while trade restrictions can undermine the efficiency of the economy. As stated in Chapter 2, the commodity or net barter terms of trade is the dimension most associated with higher exports and lower trade restrictions. As shown in Chapter 2, terms of trade is a positive determinant of economic growth. Countries in which terms of trade are greater were shown to experience greater economic growth. Given the association between economic growth and political stability, terms of trade may be hypothesized as a determinant of political risk. *Therefore, the lower the terms of trade, the higher the political risk.*

Total Expenditure in Health and Education as a Percentage of Gross Domestic Product

As shown in Chapter 2, the expenditure on health and education, as a percentage of gross domestic product, leads to lower economic growth. The result was consistent with supply risk theorists who argue that the taxes required for financing government expenditures distort incentives and reduce efficient resource allocation and the level of output. However, the same expenditures on education and health are expected to generate a healthier political climate, resulting in a better political stability and lower political risk. *Therefore, the higher the total expenditures on health and education, as a percentage of gross domestic product, the higher the political stability, measured by the political risk index.*

Military Expenditures as a Percentage of Gross National Product

Military expenditures divest resources from projects benefiting economic growth, health, and education to name only a few public interest benefits. Military expenditures are generally motivated by a desire to be strong militarily to fend off imaginary or actual enemies, to attack rightly or wrongly other countries, and most of the time are used by the rulers of a nation to subjugate their own people. Needless to say military expenditures are a deterrent to economic growth and a sure indication of an unstable or ruthless political regime. *Therefore, the higher the military expenditures, as a percentage of gross national product, the higher the political instability and the higher the political risk of a country.*

METHODOLOGY

The dependent variable used is the political risk component of the ICRG. The independent variables are (a) the human development index; (b) the gross domestic savings, as a percentage of gross domestic product; (c) the labor force, as a percentage of total population; (d) the terms of trade; (e) the total expenditures on education and health, as a percentage of gross domestic product; and (f) the military expenditure as a percentage of gross national product. The model is follows:

Exhibit 4.1
Sample of Countries

1. Australia	13. India	25. South Korea
2. Austria	14. Japan	26. Spain
3. Brazil	15. Luxembourg	27. Sweden
4. Canada	16. Malaysia	28. Switzerland
5. Colombia	17. Mexico	29. Taiwan
6. Denmark	18. Netherlands	30. Thailand
7. Egypt	19. New Zealand	31. Turkey
8. Finland	20. Norway	32. United Kingdom
9. France	21. Pakistan	33. United States
10. Germany	22. Portugal	34. Venezuela
11. Greece	23. Singapore	
12. Hong Kong	24. South Africa	

$$PR = a_0 + a_1 HDI + a_2 GDSP + a_3 LFTP + a_4 TOT$$
$$+ a_5 TEEHG + a_6 TEEHG + a_7 MEG + \mu$$

where

PR = Political risk index
HDI = Human development index
$GDSP$ = Gross domestic savings, as a percentage of gross domestic product
$LFTP$ = Labor force, as a percentage of total population
TOT = Terms of trade
$TEEHG$ = Total expenditures on education and health, as a percentage of gross domestic product.
MEG = Military expenditures, as a percentage of gross national product

The thirty-four countries chosen for analysis are shown in Exhibit 4.1 Because of data limitations, the sample was reduced later to 22 countries. The data used are shown in Exhibit 4.2.

Exhibit 4.2
Data Used

OBS	PR	HDI	GDSP	LFTP	TOT	TEEHG	MEG
1.	76.0	0.973	23	47.2	74	12.8	2.7
2.	88.0	0.957	27	47.3	98	14.4	1.3
3.	·	0.759	28	41.9	117	5.8	0.9
4.	81.0	0.983	23	50.3	119	15.8	2.2
5.	60.0	0.757	22	43.7	68	3.6	1.0
6.	86.0	0.967	21	55.2	107	13.3	2.1
7.	·	0.34	8	31.6	62	6.6	8.9
8.	85.0	0.963	27	51.1	114	13.1	1.7
9.	79.0	0.971	21	45.0	101	15.2	3.9
10.	83.5	0.959	26	50.3	106	12.7	3.1
11.	·	0.934	11	38.2	89	8.4	5.7
12.	58.0	0.934	33	49.7	105	·	·
13.	·	0.308	21	37.9	119	4.3	3.5
14.	65.0	0.955	23	40.4	108	10.8	2.3
15.	80.0	0.993	33	50.0	157	13.3	1.0
16.	63.0	0.884	38	42.1	108	3.4	5.2
17.	93.0	0.954	·	42.8	·	10.3	0.8
18.	71.0	0.802	36	43.8	74	9.7	6.1
19.	71.0	0.838	23	38.4	67	4.5	0.6
20.	85.0	0.976	23	41.2	91	15.3	3.1
21.	78.0	0.959	26	45.9	110	11.8	2.2

No.	PR	HDI	LFTP	GDSP	TOT	TEEHG	MEG
22.	87.0	0.978	28	50.0	67	14.2	3.2
23.	.	0.311	13	28.8	106	2.4	3.3
24.	69.0	0.879	.	45.6	107	10.5	6.7
25.	79.0	0.879	41	48.6	101	6.3	5.5
26.	.	0.766	25	36.0	73	5.2	3.9
27.	.	0.951	22	36.3	103	9.2	2.3
28.	81.0	0.982	21	51.4	95	16.5	2.9
29.	93.0	0.981	31	49.2	103	12.9	1.9
30.	71.0	.	.	.	.	.	.
31.	57.0	0.713	26	52.5	82	4.2	4.0
32.	.	0.694	26	38.5	115	3.3	4.9
33.	76.0	0.967	17	48.6	93	11.1	5.0
34.	78.0	0.976	13	48.9	118	18.0	6.7
35.	75.0	0.848	25	35.9	41	6.5	1.6

PR = Political Risk; HDI = Human Development Index; GDSP = Gross Domestic Savings as a Percentage of Gross Domestic Product; LFTP = Labor Force as a Percentage of Total Population; TOT = Terms of Trade; TEEHG = Total Expenditures on Education and Health as a Percentage of Gross Domestic Product; MEG = Military Expenditures as a Percentage of Gross National Product.

RESULTS

Exhibits 4.3 and 4.4 show, respectively, the sample statistics and the Pearson correlation coefficients. The evidence, shown in Exhibit 4.5, reveals that political risk as measured by the ICRG political risk index is positively related to (a) the human development index; (b) the gross domestic savings, as a percentage of gross domestic product; (c) the labor force, as a percentage of total population; and (d) the total expenditures on education and health, as a percentage of gross domestic product and negatively related to (a) the terms of trade and (b) the military expenditures, as a percentage of gross national product. All the hypotheses in the study are verified. Basically, the higher the political risk, the lower the human development index, the lower the labor force as a percentage of total population, the lower the gross domestic savings as a percentage of gross domestic product, and the lower the total expenditures on education and health, as a percentage of gross domestic product. Similarly, the higher the political risk, the higher the terms of trade and the higher the military expenditure, as a percentage of gross national product. Exhibit 4.6 shows the actual and predicted political risk ratings for the 22 countries. Although the actual and predicted values differ, the analysis does not result in aberrant predictions.

CONCLUSION

The purpose of this chapter was to replicate the ICRG political risk index on the basis of economic and political variables proposed in the theoretical and empirical literature on the determinants of political risk. The evidence reveals that political risk measured by the ICRG political risk index responds to all the variables proposed with the exact sign. Basically the level of the United Nations human development index; the gross domestic savings, as a percentage of gross domestic product; the labor force, as a percentage of total population, and the total expenditures on health and education, as a percentage of gross do-

ample Statistics

ariable	N	Mean	Std Dev	Sum	Minimum	Maximum
R	27	76.6111	9.9984	2069	57.0000	93.0000
DI	34	0.8572	0.1855	29.1450	0.3080	0.9930
DSP	32	24.4063	7.3347	781.0000	8.0000	41.0000
TP	34	44.2441	6.3792	1504	28.8000	55.2000
T	33	96.9091	22.3220	3198	41.0000	157.0000
EHG	33	9.8606	4.5303	325.4000	2.4000	18.0000
EG	33	3.3394	2.0228	110.2000	0.6000	8.9000

xhibit 4.4
orrelation Table

Pearson Correlation coefficients / Prob > | R | under $H_0 : RH_0 = 0$

	PR	HDI	GDSP	LFTP	TOT	TEEHG	MEG
R	1.00000	0.68148	-0.11946	0.22707	0.19903	0.67035	-0.30135
	0.0	0.0001	0.5782	0.2646	0.3402	0.0002	0.1432
	27	26	24	26	25	25	25
DI		1.00000	0.31939	0.65051	0.13673	0.70307	-0.29348
		0.0	0.0748	0.0001	0.4480	0.0001	0.0974
		34	32	34	33	33	33
DSP			1.00000	0.38391	0.17925	-0.06811	-0.25530
			0.0	0.0301	0.3263	0.7158	0.1657
			32	32	32	31	31
TP				1.00000	0.30843	0.62417	-0.18002
				0.0	0.0808	0.0001	0.3161
				34	33	33	33
T					1.00000	0.25986	-0.12137
					0.0	0.1509	0.5082
					33	32	32
EHG						1.00000	-0.09653
						0.0	0.5931
						33	33
G							1.00000
							0.0
							33

Exhibit 4.5
The Determinants of Political Risk

Dependent Variable PR

Analysis of Variance

Source	DF	Sum of Squares	Mean Square	F Value	Prob>F
Model	6	1521.65988	253.60998	11.186	0.0001
Error	16	362.75316	22.67207		
C Total	22	1884.41304			

Root MSE	4.76152	R-Square	0.8075
Dep Mean	77.28261	Adj R-sq	0.7353
C.V.	6.16118		

Parameter Estimates

Variable	DF	Parameter Estimate	Standard Error	T for H_0: Parameter = 0	Prob >|T|
INTERCEPT	1	-10.281884	23.85980313	-0.431	0.6723
HDI	1	63.103908	26.95574846	2.341	0.0325
GDSP	1	0.561722	0.18731334	2.999	0.0085
LFTP	1	0.435851	0.26252862	1.660	0.1163
TOT	1	-0.154276	0.05808353	-2.656	0.0173
TEEHG	1	1.105056	0.51673719	2.139	0.0482
MEG	1	-1.120916	0.62216954	-1.802	0.0905

mestic product negatively affect the political risk rating. In addition, the level of the terms of trade and the level of military expenditures, as a percentage of gross domestic product, positively affect the political risk rating. The model is not only explanatory but predictive of political risk.

Exhibit 4.6
Actual and Predicted Political Risk Ratings

Obs	Dep Var PR	Predict Value	Residual
1.	76.0000	84.3118	-8.3118
2.	88.0000	85.2274	2.7726
3.	.	58.9546	.
4.	81.0000	83.2272	-2.2272
5.	60.0000	61.2589	-1.2589
6.	86.0000	82.4305	3.5695
7.	.	20.5998	.
8.	85.0000	82.9089	2.0911
9.	79.0000	79.2449	-0.2449
10.	83.5000	80.9690	2.5310
11.	.	60.6483	.
12.	58.0000	.	.
13.	.	19.9388	.
14.	65.0000	73.2051	-8.2051
15.	80.0000	82.0647	-2.0647
16.	63.0000	66.4634	-3.4634
17.	93.0000	.	.
18.	71.0000	72.1048	-1.1048
19.	71.0000	66.2192	4.7808
20.	85.0000	81.5776	3.4224
21.	78.0000	78.4484	-0.4484
22.	87.0000	90.7229	-3.7229
23.	.	11.7982	.
24.	69.0000	.	.
25.	79.0000	74.6144	4.7808
26.	.	57.9020	.
27.	.	69.6072	.
28.	81.0000	86.2116	-5.2116
29.	93.0000	86.7154	6.2846
30.	71.0000	.	.
31.	57.0000	59.7051	-2.7051
32.	.	45.3098	.
33.	76.0000	73.7851	2.2149
34.	78.0000	74.0994	3.9006
35.	75.0000	71.9844	3.0156

APPENDIX: THE HUMAN DEVELOPMENT INDEX

Beginning in 1990, the UN human development index is composed of the three indices of life expectancy, education, and income. Three steps are used to construct the HDI. First, a maximum and a minimum value of each of these basic variables—life expectancy (X1), literacy (X2), and (the log of) per capital GDP (X3)—are defined for each country. A deprivation indicator for the *j*th country with respect to the *i*th variable is defined:

$$Iij = \frac{(Max\ Xij\ -\ Xij)}{(Max_{I}\ Xij\ -\ min\ Xij)}$$

Second, an average deprivation indicator (*Ij*), computed from the simple average of the three indicators, is

$$Ij = \frac{1}{3}\ E\ Iij$$

Third, the HDI is computed as one minus the average deprivation index:

$$(HDI)j = (1\ -\ Ij)$$

The following example illustrates the computation of the HDI for the Bahamas:

Maximum country life expectancy	= 78.6
Minimum country life expectancy	= 42.0
Maximum country educational attainment	= 70.1
Minimum country educational attainment	= 9.1
Maximum country adjusted real GDP per capita	= 5,070
Minimum country adjusted real GDP per capita	= 350
Bahamas life expectancy	= 71.5
Bahamas educational attainment	= 68.1
Bahamas adjusted GDP per capita	= 4,997
Bahamas life expectancy deprivation = (78.6 − 71.5) / (78.6 − 42.0)	= 0.193
Bahamas educational attainment deprivation = (70.1 − 68.1) / (70.1 − 9.1)	= 0.032
Bahamas GDP deprivation	

= (5,070 − 4,997) / (5,070 − 350)   = 0.015

Bahamas average deprivation
  = (0.193 + 0.032 + 0.015) / 3   = 0.080

Bahamas human development index (HDI)
  = 1 − 0.080   = 0.920

NOTES

1. C. I. Plossner, "The Search for Growth," in *Policies for Long Run Economics* (Kansas City: Federal Reserve Bank of Kansas, 1992), pp. 57–86.

2. R. Solov, "A Contribution to the Theory of Economic Growth," *Quarterly Journal of Economics* 3 (1956), p. 70.

3. W. W. Rostow, *The Stages of Economic Growth: A Noncommunist Manifesto* (London: Cambridge University Press, 1960).

4. S. Rebelo, "Long-run Policy Analysis and Long-term Growth," *Journal of Political Economy* 99 (1991), pp. 500–521.

5. R. J. Barro, "Economic Growth in a Cross Section of Countries," *Quarterly Journal of Economics* (May 1991), pp. 407–444.

6. Edgar O. Edwards, *Employment in Developing Countries: Report on a Ford Foundation Study* (New York: Columbia University Press, 1974), pp. 10–11.

7. Lewis [first name unknown], "Economic Development with Unlimited Supplies of Labor," 1961. The model was formalized and extended in J. C. H. Fei and G. Ramis, "A Theory of Economic Development," *American Economic Review* 51 (1961), pp. 326–352.

8. Michael P. Todaro, "A Model of Labor Migration and Urban Unemployment in Less Developed Countries," *American Economic Review*, 59, 1 (1969), pp. 138–148.

9. Michael P. Todaro, *Economic Development in the Third World* (New York: Longman, 1985), pp. 244–245.

10. Felipe Pazos, "Regional Integration of Trade among Less Developed Countries: A Survey of Research," *Journal of Economic Literature*, 8, 2 (1970), p. 374

11. P. P. Streeten, "Trade Strategies for Development: Some Themes for the Seventies," *World Development* 1, 6 (June 1973), p. 1.

12. Ibid., p. 2.

13. Ibid.

SELECTED READINGS

Cosset, Jean-Claude, and Jean Roy. "The Determinants of Country Risk Ratings." *Journal of International Business Studies* 22, 1 (1991), pp. 135–142.

Riahi-Belkaoui, Ahmed. *Accounting in the Developing Countries*. Westport, CT: Quorum Books, 1994.

Todaro, Michael P. *Economic Development in the Third World*. New York: Longman, 1985.

5

Managing Political Risk

INTRODUCTION

This chapter deals with the management of political risk in an international context characterized by a game between firms and host countries. The management of political risk calls first for a prediction of political risk using the model introduced in Chapter 4 before proceeding with various alternatives to cope with political risk, reduce political vulnerability and risk, account for political risk, and manage terrorist threats.

THE GAME IN INTERNATIONAL BUSINESS

Multinational corporations need to approach the problem of imposition of controls over international business as a vast international game, involving players, moves, strategies, and payoffs.[1] The players are the firms and the host countries. The objectives are a practical maximization of the present value of expected cash flows for the firms and maximization of net national benefits for the countries. The strategies that can be used by either firms or countries can be based on the following simplified sequence of play:

1. International firms locate business activity for a "practical maximization" of expected net cash flow subject to allowances for the risk of potential controls.

2. Countries alter controls to maximize natural benefits, bearing in mind the likely reactions of firms and ultimate reactions of other countries.

3. Firms realign existing operations and redirect new investment in the light of changed controls.

4. Other countries feel indirect effects of the changed controls and move to alter their own controls.[2]

The key is to be able to predict steps 2 and 4 using the political risk prediction model advocated in this book, and to map the right course of action. In mapping the right course of action, the multinational firm needs to identify the major nationalist issues and the political opportunities they may present. As shown in Exhibit 5.1, nationalist issues can be viewed as an aggregate of the three distinct but often interwined elements: national interest, national sovereignty, and national identity.[3] Each issue entails a host country position and a firm's position as well as political opportunities for the foreign firm. It is these political opportunities that should map the strategies of the firm in planning the political game. Accordingly, a matrix analysis of the political game is presented in Exhibit 5.2. It involves specific actions in the functional areas of management, finance, marketing, and production needed to counter the political issues of national interest, national sovereignty, and national identity.

PREDICTING POLITICAL RISK

The prediction of political risk is the most important step in the management of political risk. Firms need to make use of a political forecasting model that assesses political risk. Before the application of the model, firms need to place the investment risk in a useful framework for political risk evaluation. An example

Exhibit 5.1
Major Nationalist Issues

Nationalist issues	Host country criticizes:	Foreign company criticizes:	Political opportunities:
NATIONAL INTEREST	The behavior of foreign companies that does not actively promote, is inconsistent with, or goes against the economic and social goals of the host country;	The behavior of host governments that amounts to a mistaken notion of the national interest or to the faulty implementation of economic and social goals;	The foreign company can actively participate in the development of the host country;
NATIONAL SOVEREIGNTY	The behavior of foreign corporations that reduces the actual (or potential) control over the nation's development, as revealed by their allegiance to their home country policies, as well as the potential lack of control over the foreign corporation's policies in the host country;	The refusal of host governments to accept supranational agreements regarding the handling of disputes or to abide by such international agreements.	The foreign company can play off the demands of the host country against those of its home government;
NATIONAL IDENTITY	The lack of (or the uncertain) loyalty of foreign companies as revealed by their lack of understanding of and concern for the local desire to be independent and "different."	The discrimination by host governments against foreign companies simply because the latter are foreign.	The foreign company can develop policies and practices compatible with local conditions, ways and aspirations.

Source: Jean Boddewyn and Etienne F. Cracco, "The Political Game in World Business," *Columbia Journal of World Business* (May–February 1972), p. 48. Copyright 1972. Reprinted with permission.

Exhibit 5.2
Matrix Analysis of the Political Game

Political Issues ↓ / Corporations Functional Areas →	Management	Finance	Marketing	Production
NATIONAL INTEREST	—reduction of unemployment —training of managerial talents —training of skilled workers	—inflow of new permanent capital —improvement of the balance of trade and payments —increase of public revenue	—satisfaction of demand —substitute for imports	—creation of a local production base, as efficient as possible —creation of backward and forward links (suppliers, customers, service firms)
NATIONAL SOVEREIGNTY	—limitation of foreign personnel into managerial and highly technical positions —representation of nationals on board of directors	—increase of local capital participation into a control position —control of investment policy by channeling capital into high-priority projects	—development of exports and control over their destination	—generation of self-sufficiency —research and development designed to more continuous operations
NATIONAL IDENTITY	—development of local personnel up to 100%	—control over local borrowings —reinvestment of all local earnings —discriminatory incentives	—create local products and markets	—development of production facilities owned by local nationals —local processes designed to reflect local resources

Source: Jean Boddewyn and Etienne F. Cracco, "The Political Game in World Business," *Columbia Journal of World Business* (May–February 1972), p. 53. Copyright 1972. Reprinted with permission.

of a good political risk evaluation framework is presented in Exhibit 5.3. It includes 10 variables that need ratings, including six internal causes of stress, two external causes of stress, and two symptoms.[4]

The six internal causes of stress are

1. Factionalization of the political spectrum and the power of these factions;
2. Factionalization by language, ethnic, and/or religious groups and the power of these factions;
3. Restrictive (coercive) measures required to retain power;
4. Mentality, including xenophobia, nationalism, corruption, nepotism, and willingness to compromise;
5. Social conditions, including extremes in population density and the distribution of wealth; and
6. Organization and strength of forces for a radical left government.

The two external causes of stress are

1. Dependence on or importance to a hostile major power and
2. Negative influence of regional political forces.

The two symptoms are

1. Societal conflict and
2. Political instability.

A political risk model can be developed as the basis of these variables. The 10 variables are rated from 0 to 70 for three periods, leading to a range of 0 for no political risk to 70 for completely prohibitive risk. Thirty points can be added to causes that should be given additional weight because of their impact on overall political risk. Four categories emerge:

1. Minimal risk: 0–19 rating points.
2. Acceptable risk: 20–34 rating points.

Exhibit 5.3
A Framework for Political Risk Evaluation

CAUSES

— Internal —→

Fractionalization of the political spectrum and power of resulting factions	Fractionalization by language, ethnic, or religious groups and power of resulting factions	Restrictive measures required to retain power	Xenophobia, nationalism, and inclination to compromise
0 - 7	0 - 7	0 - 7	0 - 7

SYMPTOMS

External →

136

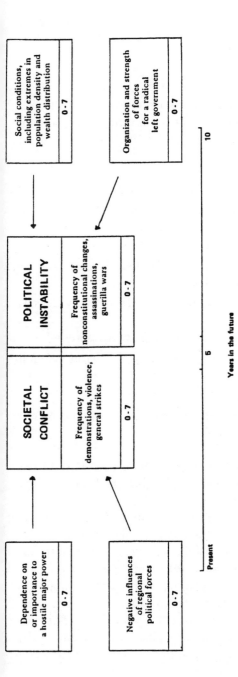

Source: Reprinted from F. T. Haner, "Rating Investment Risks Abroad," *Business Horizons* (April 1979), p. 20. Copyright 1979 by the Foundation for the School of Business at Indiana University. Used with permission.

137

3. High risk: 35–44 rating points.
4. Prohibitive risk: over 45 rating points.[5]

One way of predicting political risk is to analyze specific risk vulnerability by questioning whether the project or the product is strongly tied to natural goals. The following questions can be invaluable in the analysis:

Do nationals have the capability to operate the business successfully?

Are the foreign firm and its foreign managers highly visible in the local setting?

Are periodic external inputs of new technology required?

Will the project be competing strongly with local nationals who are in or are trying to enter the same field?

Is the operation dependent on natural resources, particularly minerals or oil?

Does the investment put pressure on balance of payments?

Does the enterprise have a strong monopoly position in the local market?

Is the product socially essential and acceptable?

Does a social cost-benefit analysis of the project show attractive and continuing benefits to the country?

In general, projects or products that contribute strongly to national goals are likely to receive favorable political attention when first initiated.[6]

In addition, the multinational firm needs to better know its publics from which criticisms may come and the issues they may frequently raise. The possible publics include (a) church, (b) labor, (c) suppliers, (d) customers, (e) competitors, (f) pressure groups, (g) stockholders, (h) academia, (i) the general public, (j) minority groups, (k) public media, (l) governments and agencies, (m) conservationists, and (n) the financial community.[7] Some of the issues of interest to these publics include (a) nationalism, (b) industrial democracy, (c) environment protection, (d) energy and raw materials, (e) taxes, (f) incentives and restrictions, (g) investment approvals and permits, (h) personnel relations, (i) attracting personnel, (j) merger and acquisitions, (k) money and credit, (l) legitimacy, (m) prices and profits, (n) image (company and product), (o) consumerism, (p) women's liberation, (q) union relations, and (r) equal opportunities.[8]

The way of predicting political risk advocated in this book is to rely on the political risk model developed in Chapter 4. The model is as follows:

$$PR = -10.281 + 63.103HDI + 0.561GDSP + 0.435LFTP \\ - 0.154TOT + 1.105TEEHG - 1.120MEG$$

where

$$
\begin{aligned}
PR &= \text{Political risk} \\
HDI &= \text{Human development index} \\
GDSP &= \text{Gross domestic saving, as a percentage of gross} \\
&\quad \text{domestic product} \\
LFTP &= \text{Labor force, as a percentage of total population} \\
TOT &= \text{Terms of trade} \\
TEEHG &= \text{Total expenditures on education and health, as a} \\
&\quad \text{percentage of gross domestic product} \\
MEG &= \text{Military expenditures, as a percentage of} \\
&\quad \text{gross national product.}
\end{aligned}
$$

COPING WITH POLITICAL RISK

Forecasting political risk is not enough; the problem is how to cope and live with it or how to minimize it. Various techniques have been proposed for minimizing it. Eiteman and Stonehill suggested the following three categories of techniques for dealing with political risk:

1. Negotiating the environment before investment by concluding concession agreements, adaptation to host country goals, planned investment, and investment guarantees.

2. Implementing specific operating strategies after the investment decision in production, logistics, marketing, finance, organization, and personnel. For example, local zoning, a safe location of facilities, and control of transportation and of patents and processes are examples of operating strategies in production and logistics that may reduce the likelihood of political interference or expropriation.

3. Resorting to specific compensation strategies after expropriation, including rational negotiation, application of power tactics to bargaining legal remedies, use of the International Center for Settlement of Investment Disputes, and surrenders in the interest of seeking salvage.[9]

Another way of coping with political risk is to negotiate a tight investment agreement that spells out the specific rights and responsibilities of both the foreign firm and the host government. Eiteman and Stonehill suggested that the investment agreement spell out, among other things, the following policies on financial and managerial issues:

- The basis on which fund flows, such as dividends, management fees, and loan repayments, may be remitted;
- The basis for setting any applicable transfer prices;
- Obligations to build, or fund, social and economic overhead projects, such as schools, hospital, and retirement systems;
- Methods of taxation, including the rate, the type of taxation, and how the rate base is determined;
- Access to host country capital markets, particularly for long-term borrowing;
- Permission for 100 percent foreign ownership versus required local ownership (joint venture) participation;
- Price controls, if any, applicable to sales in the host country markets;
- Requirements for local sourcing versus import of raw materials and components;
- Permission to use expatriate managerial and technical personnel; and
- Provision for arbitration of disputes.[10]

Haendel classified, appropriately, the traditional tools of risk management into five general categories:

1. Avoidance, whereby the risk manager may recommend not investing or diversifying, or else impose a ceiling on the exposure a firm allows a country.

2. Transfer, whereby the risk manger may recommend including local individuals as either investors, or managers.

3. Diversification and loss prevention, whereby the risk manger may recommend diversifying to reduce the reliance on a production facility of natural resource supply in any one country.

4. Insurance, whereby the risk manager may recommend that the firm secures insurance against political risk as a way of shielding the firm's asset from unexpected losses. This may even include self-insurance in the form of a separate fund.

5. Retention, whereby the risk manager may recommend that not all political risks can be avoided, transferred, diversified, or insured against. In such a case the firm should include political risk analysis in its decision-making process.[11]

It remains to know what the multinationals actually do to cope with political risk. A study prepared for the Financial Executives Research Foundation surveyed multinationals and found a number of techniques that could be used both before the investment and when operating overseas.[12] The techniques found to be most useful by participant firms in their preinvestment negotiations with local business, once the investment had been made and the firms were committed, were maximizing the use of local debt and local funding, adapting to changing governmental priorities, sourcing locally to stimulate the economy and to reduce dependence on imports, and increasing exports. Besides using these techniques, the respondent firms admitted to insuring against the losses that might be caused by expropriation/confiscation, nationalization, foreign exchange, inconvertibility, war, revolution or insurrection damages, kidnaping and ransom, long-term currency losses, and even inflation. The insurance was provided by the Overseas Private Investment Corporation (OPIC), a credit insurance program administered by the Export/Import Bank of the United States (Eximbank) jointly with Foreign Credit Insurance Association (FCIA), and private political risk insurance organizations like the American International Group (AIG) and Lloyd's of London.

In fact, insurance coverage for multinational corporations can be obtained from a number of sources, including

a. Private insurance;
b. Government insurance, both OPIC and FCIA; and
c. The Multilateral Investment Guarantee Agency (MIGA).

MIGA was created in 1988 to help its more than 100 members create an attractive investment climate, as coinsurer with, or a reinsurer of, other insurers. It offers the following four basic types of coverage: currency transfer, expropriation, war and civil disturbances, and breach of contract. They are defined as follows:

Currency transfer coverage protects against losses arising from an inability to convert local currency returns into foreign exchange for transfer outside the host country.

Expropriation coverage protects against loss as a result of acts by the host government that may reduce or eliminate ownership of, control over, or rights to, the insured investment.

War and civil disturbances coverage protects against losses arising as a result of any military action or civil disturbance that destroys or damages tangible assets of the project enterprise or interferes with it operations (e.g., those resulting from politically motivated events of revolution, insurrection, coup d'état, sabotage, and terrorism).

Breach of contract coverage protects against losses arising from the investor being unable to obtain and/or enforce a decision or award against a host country that has repudiated or breached an investment contract.[13]

Exhibit 5.4 describes the MIGA guarantee process.

Exhibit 5.4
The MIGA Guarantee Process

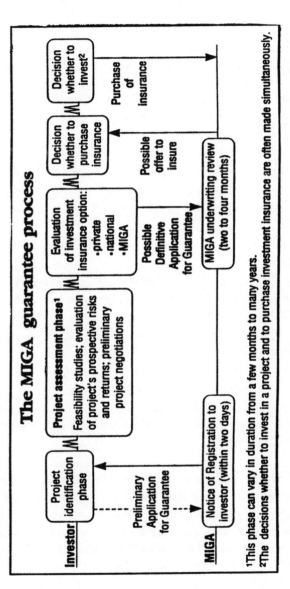

The MIGA guarantee process

Investor

Project identification phase → Project assessment phase[1]
Feasibility studies; evaluation of project's prospective risks and returns; preliminary project negotiations → Evaluation of investment insurance option:
- private
- national
- MIGA → Decision whether to purchase insurance → Decision whether to invest[2]

Preliminary Application for Guarantee

Possible Definitive Application for Guarantee

Purchase of insurance

MIGA

Notice of Registration to investor (within two days)

MIGA underwriting review (two to four months)

Possible offer to insure

[1]This phase can vary in duration from a few months to many years.
[2]The decisions whether to invest in a project and to purchase investment insurance are often made simultaneously.

Source: Laura Wallace, "MIGA: Up and Running," *Finance & Development* (March 1992), p. 48. Reprinted with permission.

REDUCING POLITICAL VULNERABILITY AND RISK

Multinational firms have to be sensitive to the fear in most developing countries that they are being exploited for their labor, markets, or raw materials. One way of reducing political vulnerability is for the company to signal that it intends to be a good corporate citizen.[14] The following points need to be remembered by the firm:

1. The firm is a guest in the country and should act accordingly.
2. The profits of an enterprise are not solely any company's; the local national employees and the economy of the country should also benefit.
3. It is not wise to try to win over new customers by completely Americanizing them.
4. Although English is an accepted language overseas, a fluency in the language of the international customer goes far in marking sales and cementing good public relations.
5. The firm should try to contribute to the country's economy and culture with worthwhile public projects.
6. The firm should train its executives and their families to act appropriately in the foreign environment.
7. It is best not to conduct business from the United States but to staff foreign offices with competent nationals and supervise the operations from home.[15]

Joint ventures with locals or local firms, expanding the investment base to include influential banks as investors, controlling the marketing and distribution, licensing technology for a fee, and planned domestication are more of the other alternatives to lessen political risk.[16] Domestication entails (a) transferring some or all of the ownership to locals, (b) promoting large number of locals to upper management, (c) giving more decision-making powers to locals, (d) producing locally rather than importing a greater number of parts, and (e) increasing export reputation toward participation in world markets.[17] Other suggestions for risk reduction strategies includes (a) relying on local partners with excellent contacts, (b) achieving a status of indispensability when having exclusive access to high technology or specific products, (c) integrating vertically offering economies of scale to the local operation, (d) local borrowing instead of bringing foreign exchange to a host country, (e) minimizing fixed investments, and (f) buying political risk insurance.[18]

ACCOUNTING FOR POLITICAL RISK

Accounting for political risk calls for a systematic approach to the assignment of a risk premium to a return-on-investment (ROI) budget. One approach consists of adjusting the corporate ROI by a numerical risk index developed for each country of operation. For example, assume that the Mantis company wholly owns three affiliates in countries A, B, and C. For the first year, the actual divisional income and investment of each affiliate are as follows:

Division	Total Investment	Divisional Income
A	$1,000,000	$200,000
B	$5,000,000	$1,550,000
C	$2,200,000	$550,000

The Mantis company requires an 8 percent return on its investments locally. In evaluating its foreign affiliates, the Mantis company relied on a political risk instrument containing 40 risk attributes. The scores for countries A, B, and C are as follows:

Country	Political Risk Index
A	20
B	10
C	12

The adjusted ROIs are computed as follows:

Division	Nominal ROI	Country Risk Coefficient	Risk-Adjusted ROI	Actual ROI
A	8%	20/40 = 0.50	0.08/0.50 = 0.16	0.20
B	8%	10/40 = 0.25	0.08/0.25 = 0.32	0.31
C	8%	12/40 = 0.30	0.08/0.30 = 0.26	0.25

Other things being equal, the best performance is obtained by the affiliate in country A.

MANAGING TERRORIST THREATS

Various measures can be used by multinational firms to minimize political risks, including (a) stimulating the local economy, (b) employing nationals, (c) sharing ownership, (d) being civic minded, (e) being politically neutral, (f) lobbying behind the scenes, and (g) observing the political mood and reducting exposure.[19] Multinationals can also keep a low profile and try to adopt a local personality. Above all, firms need to adopt corporate programs for managing terrorist threats. Terrorist threats are a reality in international business as evidenced by (a) their number two rankings as a concern of executives[20] and (b) their logistic successes—bombings, 87 percent; hostage missions, 76 percent, and assassinations, 75 percent.[21] Multinational corporations need to develop a proactive, systematic program for dealing with terrorists by identifying key events and those individuals responsible for managing each stage of terrorists' attacks.[22]

A taxonomy of a typical terrorist act is depicted in Exhibit 5.5, identifying a precrisis phase, a crisis phase, and a postcrisis phase. A survey of formal organizational programs designed to deal with terrorism identified the following program characteristics: (a) purchase of security devices and equipment (i.e., the

Exhibit 5.5
A Taxonomy of Terrorist Crises

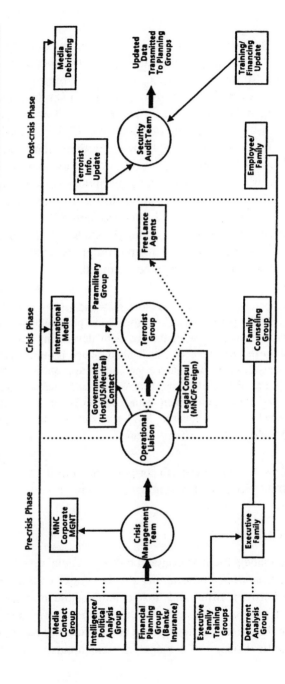

Source: Michael G. Harvey, ''A Survey of Corporate Programs for Managing Terrorist Threats,'' *Journal of International Business Studies* 24, 3 (1993), p. 468. Reprinted with permission.

means to protect executives and assets); (b) training of executives; (c) training of middle managers and foreign national employees; (d) protection of assets; (e) training of families; (f) allocation of dollars to terrorist security planning; and (g) collection of data worldwide on terrorist activities.[23] Activities included in training include (a) defensive driving, (b) self-defense, (c) preparation of information (i.e., pertinent data and files), (d) avoidance of kidnaping, (e) negotiation on the part of others (i.e., negotiating skills), (f) handling weapons, (g) collecting information from local sources on terrorists, (h) protection of assets, and (i) behavior during and after kidnaping.[24]

The reality is that less than 30 percent of the multinational corporations surveyed had formal programs to deal with a terrorist attack. The reasons cited included:

(1) Companies believe they are too small and are not important enough to be a target for terrorists; (2) terrorism is a passing trend and therefore they do not need to be concerned with developing a systematic approach to the problem; (3) the United States government and/or the foreign government will handle the corporate problems with terrorists; (4) it is too difficult to protect against possible terrorist attacks; even the United States government cannot protect government facilities; and (5) it would cost too much to develop a comprehensive system to protect executives and assets worldwide.[25]

Needless to say, these concerns do not eliminate the need for corporate programs for managing terrorist threats.

CONCLUSIONS

The management of political risk is a crucial task for managers of multinational corporations. In a context characterized by a game between firms and host countries, the managers need to predict political risk and then apply alternative means to cope with political risk, reduce political vulnerability and risk, account for political risk, and manage terrorist threats.

NOTES

1. Stephan H. Robock and Kenneth Simmonds, *International Business and Multinational Enterprises* (Homewood, IL: Richard D. Irwin, 1983).

2. Ibid., pp. 356–357.

3. Jean Boddewyn and Etienne F. Cracco, "The Political Game in World Business," *Columbia Journal of World Business* (January–February 1972), pp. 45–56.

4. F. T. Haner, "Rating Investment Risks Abroad," *Business Horizons* (April 1979), pp. 18–23.

5. Ibid., p. 22.

6. Robock and Simmonds, *International Business and Multinational Enterprises*, p. 354.

7. "How Embattled MNCs Can Devise Strategies for External Affairs," *Business International* (December 12, 1975), p. 394.

8. Ibid.

9. D. K. Eiteman and A. I. Stonehill, *Multinational Business Finance* (Reading, MA: Addison-Wesley, 1989), pp. 203–223.

10. Ibid., p. 503.

11. Dan Haendel, *Foreign Investments and the Management of Political Risk* (Boulder, CO: Westview Press, 1979), pp. 139–146.

12. Charles M. Newman II and I. James Czechowicz, *International Risk Management* (Morristown, NJ: Financial Executive Research Foundation, 1983), p. 81.

13. Laura Wallace, "MIGA: Up and Running," *Finance & Development* (March 1992), pp. 48–49.

14. Philip R. Cateora, *International Marketing*, 8th ed. (Homewood, IL: Richard D. Irwin, 1993).

15. Ibid., p. 175.

16. Ibid., pp. 176–179.

17. Philip R. Cateora, *International Marketing*, 5th ed. (Homewood, IL: Richard D. Irwin, 1983), p. 165.

18. Jean-Pierre Jeannet and Hubert D. Hennessey, *Global Marketing Strategies* (Boston: Houghton Mifflin, 1992), pp. 130–132.

19. Onkvisit, Saks and John J. Shaw, *International Marketing: Analysis and Strategy*, 3rd ed. (Englewood Cliffs, NJ: Prentice-Hall, 1997), pp. 154–158.

20. Robert Maddox, ''Terrorism's Hidden Threats and the Promise for Multinational Corporations,'' *Business Horizons* 33 (1990), pp. 48–52.

21. T. Sandler, W. Enders, and H. Lapan, ''Economic Analysis Can Help Fight International Terrorism,'' *Challenge* 34 (1991), pp. 10–12.

22. M. G. Harvey, ''A Survey of Corporate Programs for Managing Terrorist Threats,'' *Journal of International Business Studies* 24 (1993), pp. 465–478.

23. Ibid., p. 471.

24. Ibid., p. 473.

25. Ibid., p. 476.

SELECTED READINGS

Cateora, Philip R. *International Marketing*, 8th ed. Homewood, IL: Richard D. Irwin, 1993.

Eiteman, D. K., and A. I. Stonehill. *Multinational Business Finance*. Reading, MA: Addison-Wesley, 1989.

''How Embattled MNCs Can Devise Strategies for External Affairs.'' *Business International* (December 12, 1975).

Jeannet, Jean-Pierre, and Hubert D. Hennessy. *Global Marketing Strategies*. Boston: Houghton Mifflin, 1992.

Onkvisit, Saks, and John J. Shaw. *International Marketing: Analysis and Strategy*. 3rd ed. Englewood Cliffs, NJ: Prentice-Hall, 1997.

Robock, Stephan H., and Kenneth Simmonds. *International Business and Multinational Enterprises*. Homewood, IL: Richard D. Irwin, 1983.

Index

About the Authors

JANICE MONTI-BELKAOUI is Department Chair, Sociology and Communication, at Dominican University. With a doctorate in sociology and research interests in international development, mass media, and related fields, she holds several awards for excellence in teaching. Among her previous Quorum books (coauthored with Ahmed Riahi-Belkaoui) are: *Fairness in Accounting* (1996), *Human Resource Valuation* (1995), and *Accounting in the Dual Economy* (1991).

AHMED RIAHI-BELKAOUI is CBA Distinguished Professor of Accounting in the College of Business Administration, University of Illinois at Chicago. Author of more than 30 Quorum books and coauthor of several more, he is also a prolific author of articles published in the major scholarly and professional journals of his field, and has served on numerous editorial boards that oversee them.

ISBN 1-56720-196-2

EAN

9 781567 201963

HARDCOVER BAR CODE